To Annette 2 gu

best wu

MEMORIES OF HEVERSHAM

A look back at an historic South Lakeland village

BY

ROGER K. BINGHAM.

Other books by Roger K. Bingham.

- Our Village (1977)

- The Church at Heversham - a history of Westmorland's oldest recorded church (1984)

- Chronicles of Milnthorpe (1987) Cicerone Press

- Lost Resort - the flow and ebb of Morecambe (1990) Cicerone Press

- Kendal - a Social History. (1995) Cicerone Press

- From Fell and Field - a history of the Westmorland County Show 1799-1999 (1999) Cicerone Press

- Memories of Milnthorpe for the Millennium: A look back at a Westmorland Village before 1950 (2000)

- Memories of Milnthorpe for The Jubilee: a look back at a South Lakeland Village during the reign of Queen Elizabeth II 1952-2002 (2002)

Moss Side Farm Yard, Heversham, Millennium Parish Boundary Walk May 2000.

Roger K. Bingham is a professional historian and prolific author whose works include nine local history books. Born in 1942, the son of a doctor, his first home at Marsdene, Milnthorpe was situated in the civil parish of Milnthorpe and also in the ecclesiastical parish of Heversham - so he claims to belong to both places. He attended Heversham C of E School ('Leasgill School') and Heversham Grammar School (now part of Dallam School) before going on to the Universities of Cambridge and Nottingham. As a Senior Teacher he taught for 30 years mainly in 'tough' schools. He is well known in the public life of the North West being currently Chairman of Milnthorpe Parish Council, the second longest serving South Lakeland District Councillor and the Cumbria County Councillor for Lower Kentdale which includes Heversham. He holds the Culture and Communities portfolio in the Cumbria Cabinet. He is a lifelong worshipper and long time Licensed Lay Reader at Heversham Parish Church. He is donating proceeds from this book to Heversham Church to celebrate the Fiftieth Anniversary of his first becoming a Communion Server - a duty he still performs every Sunday 'at 8 a.m.'

Contents

1: Heversham In Time And Place

Ackermann's view c.1820.
Heversham is situated where the Kent estuary meanders into Morecambe Bay on the final eastward thrust of the Irish Sea. From some perspectives the ancient Church seems almost to be on the coastline.

A VIEW OF HEVERSHAM CHURCH.
Taken from *A Tour on the Lakes of Westmorland* published by R. Ackermann.

The Church's Victorian Tower designed by Austin and Paley showing Heversham Marsh or 'the mosses', Milnthorpe Sands and Arnside Viaduct. The open sea may be glimpsed between Blackstone Point on the left and Humphrey Head to the right.

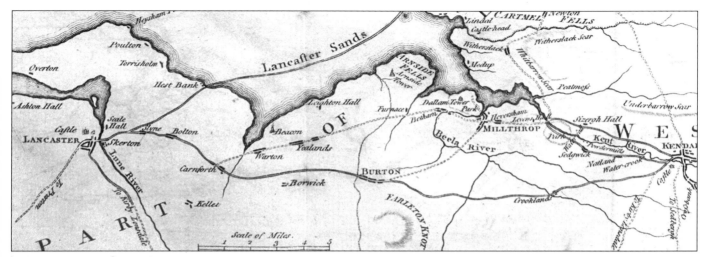

West's Map of 1789 shows Heversham's proximity to the sea. Milnthorpe ('Millthrop') was the largest place in Heversham Parish and the only port in the old County of Westmorland. Until John Macadam –allegedly of tarmac fame-built the present A6 in the 1820s the main road from Kendal to Lancaster ran through Burton-hence only tracks are indicated around Heversham.

Thus Bonnie Prince Charlie's 1745 invasion bypassed Heversham. But, revealing precautionary measures, the Church Warden's accounts for November record 'spent when the Church plate was hid' 1s and three months later 'for ringing on rejoicing Days for defeating ye Rebals 5s'.

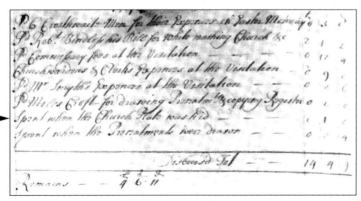

An Extract from the **Church Warden's Accounts.**

Part of the **Church Plate**-wine flagons dated 1674.

Heversham lies midway on the diagonal line running through Great Britain: both John O'Groats and Land's End are roughly 420 miles equidistant from the Parish. In 1979 a Young Variety Club sponsored roller skate for handicapped children paused at Heversham to celebrate the half-way mark. Left to right Roger Bingham, Steve Reynolds and Andy Morley, (son of theatrical impresarios Eric and Julia Morley of 'Miss World' fame) and Richard Hall-my stepfather. The skaters stayed over night with Richard and my mother, Phyllis Hall, at Fairmead.

Parish Boundary Stone at Ackenthwaite, near Milnthorpe where Heversham and Beetham Parishes met at **Paradise Lane** whose name comes from 'Parish Dyke'.

Map of the old Heversham Parish when it was one of the largest in South Westmorland stretching from Milnthorpe in the south to within two miles of Kendal in the north east and Windermere in the north west.

Boundary stone at Woodhouse marking the division with **Hincaster.**

Later stone erected at **Leasgill** to mark the boundary between Heversham and the newer **Levens** Parish.

Heversham Head rises some 412 feet (or 122.95 metres) behind the village. The building in the foreground is the **Old Grammar School** founded in 1613. The rim of Heversham's famous –or notorious - **cockpit**- can just be made out behind the school.

Me giving instructions after turning the first sod for the **Millennium Monument** on Heversham Head.

Water colour by Howard Somervell 1930 of view from the Head across the Kent's meander at Halforth –known because of its earlike shape as 'the lug'-with Whitbarrow Scar in the background.

THE LOCAL GOVERNMENT ACTS,
1888 and 1894.

TO the County Council for the Administrative County of Westmorland :

TO the Guardians of the Poor of the Kendal Union :

TO the Rural District Council of South Westmorland :

TO the Parish Council and to the Overseers of the Poor, Owners of Property, and Ratepayers of the Parish of Heversham-with-Milnthorpe :

AND to all others whom it may concern :

WHEREAS the County Council for the Administrative County of Westmorland, have made an Order, dated the 13th day of March, 1896, which provides that the existing Parish of Heversham-with-Milnthorpe shall be divided, as therein described, into two Parishes to be called respectively the Parish of Heversham and the Parish of Milnthorpe :

AND WHEREAS the Parish Council of the said Parish of Heversham-with-Milnthorpe have petitioned the Local Government Board to disallow the said Order :

AND WHEREAS the Local Government Board have directed Herbert Jenner-Fust, Junior, Esquire, one of their Inspectors, to make a Local Inquiry with a view of enabling them to determine whether the said Order should be confirmed or not :

NOTICE IS HEREBY GIVEN that the said Herbert Jenner-Fust, Junior, will attend at The Police Court, Milnthorpe, on Thursday, the Twenty-first day of May, 1896, at Ten o'clock in the Forenoon, to hold the said Local Inquiry :

AND NOTICE IS HEREBY FURTHER GIVEN that any person interested may attend at such Inquiry and be heard with reference to the proposals in the Order aforesaid, and to the said Petition :

AS WITNESS my hand this Thirteenth day of May, 1896, at the Office of the Local Government Board, Whitehall, London.

HUGH OWEN
Secretary.

Public Notice concerning the proposed division of the **Township of Heversham with Milnthorpe.**

Ruth Labsvirs admires the **Millennium Monument** which was designed by Heversham architect Paul Grout and carved by sculptors Danny and Lara Clahane.

A well wooded view of Heversham from the west c.1930. Deciduous trees grow well in the area. The Prince's Way which runs parallel to the white wall, left centre, is now a dense avenue.

Alan Wynne and John Sowerby giggle over the microscopic **Millennium Yew** planted in the churchyard in 2000.

Leasgill Tarn, c.1910. Geologically Heversham lies on boulder clay above porous limestone through which rainwater drains to a lower spring line roughly along the village street and the northern hamlet of Leasgill. Its 'gill' (or small stream) flowed into a tarn which was drained when The Prince's Way by-pass was built in 1927.

View of the Church c.1840 showing the original gates (removed to the Churchyard's west entrance in 1894) and the famous **chestnut trees** which traditionally were planted by the Rev. Dr. George Lawson, Vicar from 1797-1842.

Dr.Lawson's tomb. It is over shadowed by a huge copper beech and the conker trees. Confirming his tree planting tradition his epitaph includes: "Inter arbores aliis profuturas quas A.D.1800." (Among the trees which being for the future he planted...)

Marsh Lane 7th January 2005. The 2005 hurricane and floods (which on the same day inundated Carlisle) were the worst to hit Cumbria since 1907. Funnelling south westward directly into the tempest the Kent Estuary bore the full force of The Great Storm, so that overflowing dykes drowned the marsh fields and every road was blocked by fallen trees, entirely cutting the world off for a time.

Clearing up after The Great Storm at Hillside, Woodhouse Lane. The Douthwaites had awoken to find that their 80 foot scotch pine was lying prone across three gardens having neatly and narrowly missed neighbouring houses and most of the road.

'Down't Marsh': **Moss Side farm** from Marsh Lane c.1970.

The west wall of the **Moss Side Farm house** was rebuilt in 1977.

Tony Barnes grass tracking on the Marsh Tip. This is a raised field created in the 1950s when South Westmorland Rural District Council dumped refuse in the **former brick pond.**

Hincaster Tunnel c.1900 is part of the Lancaster to Kendal Canal opened in 1819. It is situated on the eastern edge of Heversham's ecclesiastical parish. The Moss Side brick pond provided clay for the three million bricks used in its construction.

Stacking peats near Russells Wood c.1950. From ancient times Heversham villagers enjoyed turbary or peat cutting rights on the Marsh.

Bill Strickland from Eversley Farm, Leasgill, digging peat on the mosses in 1930 and showing that cuttings could be over six feet deep.

All that FARM HOUSE, ORCHARD, GARDEN, Stable, Hayloft, Barn, Shippon, and other Outbuildings; together with about THIRTY-FIVE ACRES OF LAND, (more or less) called CROFT'S FARM, situate at Leasgill, in the Township of Levens, near Milnthorpe, now in the occupation of James Capstick, as Tenant. (This Land is in good cultivation.)

Lot VIII.

AN ALLOTMENT OF LAND, containing about ELEVEN ACRES, situate on Sampool Common, in Levens aforesaid, in good cultivation, in the occupation of John Winsgill, as Tenant.

FOUR ACRES OF PEAT MOSS, to be Sold in Lots, situate on Sampool Moss, in Levens aforesaid, and now in the occupation of Mr. Wilson, or his Under-tenants.

1823 Advert for Eversley Farm (then known as Croft's Farm) and Peat Mosses.

Peat digging on Heversham Marsh c.1920s. After drying, peats were carted to peat sheds many of which survive behind older houses. Clogs were still worn.

Illustration from **'The Lonely Plough'**, by the once famous Milnthorpe author Constance Holme. The novel centres on the devastating **Mothering Sunday Floods of 1907**. This scene showing the broken sea bankings depicts the rescue operation at College Green –although the farmhouse looks more like neighbouring Halforth 'where'd tide didn't even git int' yard'.

Waterside lies on the banks of the river Kent way out on Heversham Marsh. The farmstead, long the home of the Scott family, was called by Constance Holme **'Beautiful End'** in her novel of the same name (Mills and Boon 1918) based around the doings of farming folk 'down the mosses'.

The book cover shows the **Tattersall Armshouses** mentioned, also, on p 30. **'Looking towards the marsh and the park and the dim blueness of the bay'.**

Constance Holme riding side saddle on the 'hard land' above the estuary at about the time she wrote "The Lonely Plough" (Mills and Boon, 1914).

Frontispiece from Constance Holme's **'The Splendid Fairing'** showing the **Tidal Bore in the Kent Estuary**. In 'The Lonely Plough' she mused "the sea was always there and though it came quietly perhaps and inoffensively there would be be many a night when it would come like a beast of prey, ravening its path between narrow shores, devouring the watery desert".

Woodcut by Clare Leighton from **'The Trumpet in The Dust'** by Constance Holme (Ivor Nicholson and Watson Limited 1934) showing the heroine Mrs Clapham standing on **Heversham Head.**

Signed studio photograph of **Constance Holme c.1914.**

Arthur Nelson from Halforth Farm earned many commendations for rescuing victims from the Kent quicksands. The cross marks the spot where Arthur rescued Lt. Louis Birkett in `1946. Louis had sunk up to his armpits and Arthur only reached him in the nick of time via a ladder slung out on straw bales rolled over the oozing mud.

Arthur receives an RSPCA award for rescuing a cow. Arthur holds his certificates presented by Miss Shaw. **Sir Maurice Bromley Wilson** (Arthur's landlord) is on the right and in front is Brian Nelson with his mother Nancy.

Twenty years later Arthur, on the left, received a **Humane Society award** for saving a Milnthorpe man, Fred Gray, from the quicksands.

Near this Place are buried the Remains of JOHN HUDSON second Son of ROBERT HUDSON Elq of Tadworth Court Surry. And arfo of ISAAC HUDSON, of Long Sleddale his Schoolfellow. who were drowned bathing on the Sands the 24th of June AD.1792: both Aged 16 Years.

Memorial Plaque in Heversham Church. Despite its airy beauty Heversham Marsh can be be dangerous. The Parish Registers, monuments and gravestones record many instances of death by **'drowning on the Sands'**.

View from Leasgill looking west over the mosses. Haysteads is on the left with Bank Farm below it; the white sheds in the middle distance are piggeries at College Green while the Nelson's Halforth is 'o'er t'yonder' in the distance.

View of **Hillcrest, Leasgill** c. 1970, showing Levens village and the **Lyth Valley**. Hillcrest was built by Jim Sisson in c.1920. Subsequently he often told the tale of how when he went off to the war in 1914 his employer Mr Argles of Eversley said 'there'll be a job for you when you get back'. But, come 1919 there was no job waiting for him. So, as compensation he sold Jim a plot of land on which to build a bungalow and joiner's workshop. He built much of the house himself using timber cut from the Slacks woods while the roof was recycled from The Knoll, a chalet on Woodhouse Lane which had been blown down. Jim's family lived here until 2000 when his daughter Ray retired to Plumtree Hall. The site was then redeveloped by Robin and Ian Sisson's Priory Builders to provide four houses still owned by the Sissons. The receipt for the £25 cost of the site, which perhaps indicated the start of the family fortunes, has also been retained.

2: History Around The Church

If history is the study of the recorded past then Heversham is literally of historic significance because its ancient church was first recorded 1100 years ago.

Whitewashed Heversham in the 1860s. This is the earliest known photograph of Heversham. Historically it can be dated from between 1860 when the church clock was installed and 1869 when the old tower was demolished. Church Farm on the right has changed little in 150 years. The barn on the left was removed in 1910 to make way for a villa now known as Tower House.

Edwin Sandys Archbishop of York 1576-1588. He was briefly Vicar of Heversham c.1547. His portrait is the oldest picture of anyone connected with Heversham.

Robert Wilson Evans Vicar 1842-66.
In his day he was a distinguished writer and poet. This is the oldest available photograph of a Heversham person.

Members of the congregation in the **Kendal Torchlight procession 1980.** Left to right Lisa Casey, Elizabeth Hancock, Andrew Douthwaite, Rev. Philip Rumsey, Janet Holmes, Roger Bingham wearing an anachronistic watch. They were depicting a Viking attack on Heversham Church.

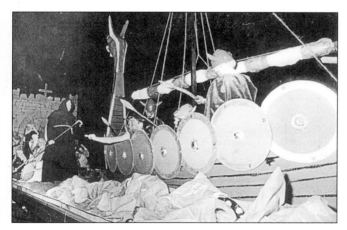

Heversham's Longboat 1980.

Map of the North West from the Oxford History 'Anglo-Saxon England' by F.M. Stenton. Heversham –**'Hefresham'**-, Penrith/ Eamont Bridge- 'aet Eamontum' and Carlisle-'Luel' are the only Cumbrian places on the map. Heversham was first recorded in c.910 A.D. in the annals of Lindisfarne which states that "Tildred, Abbot of Heversham" escaped to the North East following Viking raids on Cumbria. This early reference prompted Roger Bingham to add 'A History of **Westmorland's oldest recorded church**' to the title of his work 'The Church at Heversham' (1984).

Four sides of the Anglo-Saxon Cross shaft in the Church Porch. This 'most precious relic' dating from c.750 A.D. is all that remains of Heversham's Monastery which might have been founded by missionaries from the Irish Celtic Church in c. 600 A.D. but which did not survive the Viking incursions-though the Church did.

Ninezergh Farm in c1960 showing the meandering Kent and Whitbarrow Scar. Traditionally Ninezergh takes its name from **St. Ninian** who sailed up the Bay from the Celtic Church of Ireland to evangelise the area in the seventh century. Unlike the south of England, which had to be reconverted by St. Augustine after 597 AD, Christianity had probably lingered on in the north west since Roman times thereby making Heversham one of the oldest places in Christendom.

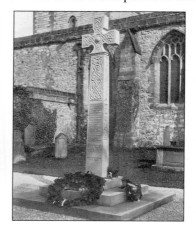

Heversham's War Memorial was designed by J.F.Curwen to resemble the Anglo-Saxon Cross. A portion of the right arm of the cross is built into the south wall of the church at window sill height just left of the buttress.

Hincaster Hall photographed about 1910 when the 16th century hall won a competition for 'England's most picturesque Farmhouse'. At that time it was part of the Argles Estate, being farmed by the Prickett family.

The 'caster' name ending is a reminder of Roman times when a branch road ran through the district connecting the main military highway in the Lune valley with Watercrook Fort near Kendal. **The first Christian** to touch Heversham may well have been an unknown legionary tramping through Hincaster perhaps with the cross of Christ surreptitiously scratched on his armour.

Heversham's war dead were: 1914-18-G.A. Wilson, J. Hamilton, T. Philipson, H.V. Shaw, J.E. Woof, J. Chamley, R. Smith, J. Atkinson, W. H. Ward, F. Baines, G.H. Proctor, E. Proctor, J. Proctor, J. Sisson, J.Moore, T. Dowker, J.B. Germaine. Curiously Proctor is spelt with an 'e' for the same names on the memorial inside the Church. In 1939-45 there was a cruel gender equality in the war dead as two of the four victims, Jean Strickland and Jean Binnie were members of the women's forces. The men were W. Norman Smith and William G. Sisson.

Hincaster Mission Room is the low building on the left seen in the snow c1940. As a 'chapel of ease' of Heversham Church, services have been held here since the 1880s.

Leading Aircrafts Woman **Jean Strickland.**

Corporal **George Proctor** who died at Allahabad, India in 1918.

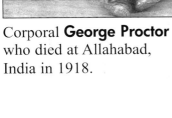

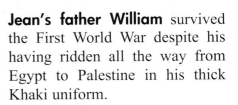

Jean's father William survived the First World War despite his having ridden all the way from Egypt to Palestine in his thick Khaki uniform.

On top of the Church tower c.1960. Left to right Jim Sisson jnr, Bill Dawson, Robin Sisson, 'Old' Jim, Ian Sisson. Unlike their relative and namesake both these J. Sissons survived their war service respectively in 1939-45 and 1914-18. But- 'Young Jim' did so 'only just.' Having parachuted into Arnhem in September 1944 he was reported as 'missing' - presumed dead. Then, at Christmas The Red Cross reported that he was still alive as a POW. To everyone's relief he returned to Heversham where he enjoyed a productive half century of 'borrowed time'.

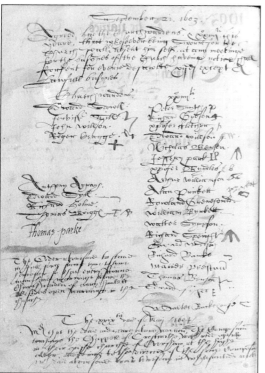

September 20 1603
Agreed by the churchwardens and 24 this year that whosoever being sworn for the churche shall not absent himself at any meeting for the business of the church having notice, shall forfeit for every default 12d. except (on) lawful business.
Churchwardens
Edward Saul
Gervase Gill
John William
Roger Cragge

Anthony Ayray
Edward Gyll
Richard Holme
Thomas Brigge
Thomas Parke

The Order above said to stand in full force from tyme to tyme hereafter so that every sworn man have warning from the churchwardens of every hamlett besides open warnings in the Churche.

29th day of Mai 1604
Mem the dai and yeare above written of the Composition touchine the Chappelle of Crosthwaite was read openly in the Parish Church of Heversham at the High altar according to the dir -ection of the same composition which day above said was Tuesday in Whitsuntide Week.

The 24
Peter Smythe
Richard Gibson
Christopher Fletcher
Edward Willson
Nicholas Benson
Jeffrey Parke
Christopher Bindloss
Arthur Willisson
Allan Prickett
Rowland Greenhowe
William Birkett
Walter Sympson
Richard Speight
Edward Willson
Richard Banks
Walter Preston
Thomas Benson
Edward Fingis

Walter Barkehouse

Translation of the 1603/4 Churchwardens Accounts

The document shows that the church was already open for services after a fire in 1601 which reportedly 'utterly consumed' the building. Even so the church was not officially re-opened until Low Sunday 1611. The term High Altar indicates that Heversham preferred the traditional 'Catholic' usage and not the official 'Protestant' terminology of 'The Holy Table'.

A page from the Churchwardens Accounts of 1603. Like the War Memorial it lists many surnames still common in the area. Significantly most of the wardens could not write but only make a mark while Edward Wilson who founded the Grammar School in 1613 did not sign at all.

The Churchwardens Bench. It is dated 1607, six years after the Church was partly burnt down 'through the foolishness of a careless workman being a plumber'. The initials stand for: E.W. –Edward Wilson, W.B.-Walter Buskell, I.A. John Audland.

The Lychgate was erected to the memory of Churchwarden **John Audland**, a medical doctor, who died on 'the eve of the feast of the purification' 1st February, 1893.

Dr. Audland.

The Church-photographed by Mac Sisson on **a snowy New Year's Eve c.1963** when his three sons were ringing in the New Year.

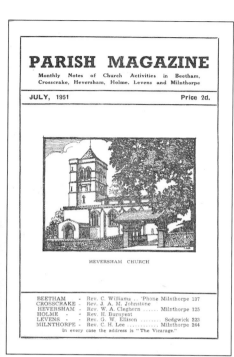

PARISH MAGAZINE

Monthly Notes of Church Activities in Beetham, Crosscrake, Heversham, Holme, Levens and Milnthorpe

JULY, 1951   Price 2d.

HEVERSHAM CHURCH

BEETHAM - Rev. C. Williams .. 'Phone Milnthorpe 137
CROSSCRAKE - Rev. J. A. M. Johnstone
HEVERSHAM - Rev. W. A. Cleghorn ...... Milnthorpe 125
HOLME - Rev. H. Burnyent
LEVENS - Rev. G. W. Ellison .... Sedgwick 223
MILNTHORPE - Rev. C. H. Lee .... Milnthorpe 244
In every case the address is "The Vicarage."

Rev. W.G. Cleghorn, Vicar 1939-1955. He taught me to be a server at Holy Communion but I did not start until Canon Lane arrived –so I've only just done 50 years in the sanctuary.

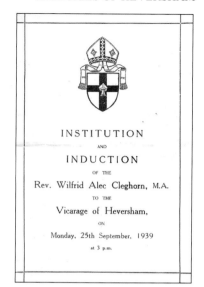

INSTITUTION
AND
INDUCTION
OF THE
Rev. Wilfrid Alec Cleghorn, M.A.
TO THE
Vicarage of Heversham,
ON
Monday, 25th September, 1939
at 3 p.m.

Service booklet for 'Cleggy's' **Induction**.

A perhaps over familiar scene on the cover of a composite **Parish Magazine** from 1951 when the Rev Wilfred Alec Cleghorn was Vicar of Heversham. Unlike his colleagues at Crosscrake and Holme he could afford a phone.

Below, **sad news** in January 1956

HEVERSHAM NOTES

Just as this magazine has gone to press, there comes the terribly sad news of the death, at the Victoria Hospital, Morecambe, of the Rev. W. A. Cleghorn, on December 27th.

Our sense of loss is so bewildering that we hardly know how to give it expression. The funeral service at Heversham Church, conducted by the Bishop of Penrith and the Rural Dean, and attended by a large number of clergy, of parishioners, and of friends from outside the parish, was a moving tribute to his memory, and to the high regard in which he is held by his very many friends.

May God comfort Mrs. Cleghorn, and all who mourn.

Except for the deletion of Christmas parties, which are cancelled, I have thought it best to leave the Vicar's notes for this magazine just as he wrote them.   C.W.

HEVERSHAM C of E SCHOOL

QUEEN ELIZABETH II

CORONATION PRIZE

awarded to

ROGER KENNETH BINGHAM.

1954

'Cleggy's' inscription in my by now very battered Bible. Canon Hancock in recent times gave out the Bibles with 'a guarantee to replace them when they wore out.' But, when I requested a replacement he said the guarantee did not apply to me 'because I had left too long ago.'

Day School. The children turned up in force and sang most beautifully in Church on the Sunday morning before the end of term. The Queen Elizabeth Coronation Prizes were awarded to Roger Bingham and John Mason. Each boy was given a special edition of the Bible, produced by the British and Foreign Bible Society in the year of its third jubilee. Roger's book is more beautifully bound than John's, but both books contain many hundreds of illustrations and maps. I hope that the books will not only be souvenirs of happy days spent in our village school, but will also be read regularly.

Extract from the Parish Magazine - September 1954. It takes a lot to embarrass me but I have always been bothered about Cleggy's awarding the leather bound Bible to me because I had 'passed my scholarship' while John got a cheaper, cloth bound version because he had not passed. Mine was the first of the **Coronation Bibles**, which, initially, were financed by funds left over from the 1953 celebrations. All leavers from what is currently called Heversham St. Peter's C. of E. Primary School now receive the same version irrespective of their scholastic performance.

Retirement of Canon Lane Vicar 1955-66 L to R. John Lathom, Norris Chamley, Mrs Lane, Canon Stanley Lane, Jim Sisson, Norman Kilshaw, Bill Dawson. The Lanes had a long retirement at Casterton, and Mrs Lane lived to be over 100.

Induction of Rev Tom Martin, Vicar 1966-75. Left to Right Churchwardens John Sowerby and Norman Kilshaw, Rev Reay, Crosscrake, Bishop Cyril Bulley, Tom Martin, ?, Churchwarden Bill Dawson, Canon Needham, Kendal.

John and Margaret Hancock at **John's final service** 31st July 2005. Margaret is holding an album of pictures illustrating their 29 years ministry in the Parish.

Canon John Hancock Vicar 1976-95 holding at her christening, in 1979, Clare Douthwaite with proud brother Andrew in attendance. At that stage the font was in its traditional place by the west door. It was subsequently moved to the front of the south aisle in order to give the congregation a better view at public baptisms.

Inside the Church c. 1900. The reference to St Mary's Church is an old mistake probably going back to before the 16th century when the church belonged to St. Mary's Abbey at York. Pevsner in his 'Buildings of England' pronounced 'the interior strikes one as Victorian' as the North Arcade, Chancel Arch and most of the fittings stem from 19th century 'restorations'. But the south arcade (right) dates from c.1180 and there are many other pre 19th century features. The hooks for the hanging oil lamps are still on the rafters. In floor space Heversham Church is the third largest out of 84 in the old county of Westmorland after Kendal and Kirkby Stephen Parish Churches.

A 'waterleaf' capital of c.**1180** on a pillar of the south arcade.

Carved respond of c.**1250** on the south arcade.

Arch and head stops to credence table of c.**1300**.

Lock on **14th century** Parish Chest.

The Dorothy Bellingham Memorial is the finest sculpture in the church. Dorothy, wife of the squire of Levens Hall, died in childbirth in 1626 aged 39 having been delivered of a dead baby depicted in swaddling clothes at her side. The epitaph tells her sad story:

Thrice six years told brought up by parents deare
Duely by them instructed in God's feare
Twice seven years more I lived to one betroth
Whose meanes in life were common to us both,
Seaven children in that space I brought
By nature perfect and of hopeful growght
His parents unto me deare as mine own
Theire loves as to ye worlds well knowne
But ere that one yeare her course had runne
God in his mercie unto me hath showne
That all theise earthly comforts are but toyes
Being compared with those celestiall joyes
Which through the blood of Christ are kept in store
For those in whome his word hath ruld before
To labour borne & by that ruld before
**To labour borne & by that forme
I bore to earth, to earth I straight was borne.**

Heversham Church. Milnthorpe.

Canon Thomas Morrell Gilbert. He was Heversham's longest serving Vicar from 1866 to 1921. When he died in London in 1928, aged 93, his remains were brought back to Heversham in a lead lined coffin that took eight men to lift.

The Churchyard c.1900. The inscription on the enclosed grave to the left of the path, just by the gate, tells of the fruitful journeys of Jane Swindlehurst who with her husband Henry 'sailed round Cape Horn in 1855 with three children and after visiting the coast of Peru returned with five children in 1859 to Hincaster House where she died in 1883'. It was amazing what the Victorians could do in a hammock.

Heversham's grandest funeral-**the burial of Sir Josceline Bagot M.P.** of Levens Hall March 1913. Canon Gilbert is at the head of the grave and the veiled widow is the dark blob to the left. 2000 mourners attended and "in order to keep space about the grave for the mourners, clergy and choir a cordon was drawn by the first Kendal Scout Troop (Lady Bagot's Own) and Heversham Grammar School Boys in charge of Mr Hamilton"-who, himself, was soon to lose his life in the imminent war.

FUNERAL OF SIR JOSCELINE BAGOT.M.P. COPYRIGHT T.E.S.

Photos of Church events provide many recent Memories of Heversham. Here we see **The Mother's Union** outside the Old School Cottage c.1985.

L to R. Back row Martha Bates, Rona Currie, Lena Rumsey, Christine Spedding, Marion Douthwaite, Eve Tilbury, John Hancock, Olive Mason, Sadie Booth, Mrs Thistlethwaite, Jenny Sisson, Nancy Tyson, Sheila Johnson, Vera McKee, Mary East, Edith Hodgson, Bobby Shackleford, Florence Cocking, Mrs Chauncey, Mona Hayton, Margaret Hancock.

In front Jean Shuttleworth, Edith Webster, Mrs Bates, Mary Davidson, Dorothy Derbyshire, Olga Pound, Visiting President of MU, Lilly Lister, Annie Proctor, Molly Wallace.

3: Through The Village

Sketch of 'Churchtown' Heversham by E. M. Edmonds c.1850.

Church Street, Milnthorpe c.1940. The Tattersall Almshouses are on the right. Heversham is joined to its big daughter of Milnthorpe by **Church Street** which, to the confusion of strangers, leads not to Milnthorpe's newer church built in 1837 but to the **'Mother Church'** of St. Peter, at Heversham. Church Street starts at the Cross Keys (St. Peter's badge) in the centre of Milnthorpe and leads north over Milnthorpe Hill to reach Heversham a mile and a half away.

Close up of the **Tattersall Almshouses.** They were built and endowed in 1884 by a wealthy brewer William Tattersall from St. Anthony's House. Although situated in Milnthorpe's Civil Parish the Almshouses and the whole of the west side of Church Street as far as Grisleymires Lane a quarter of a mile nearer Milnthorpe are in Heversham's ecclesiastical parish. My first home 'Marsdene', Milnthorpe was built in the 1930s, along with other houses, in Kirkgate Field on the top left of the picture. Thus I claim to be a native of both Heversham and Milnthorpe-but it also gives both places the excuse to disown me.

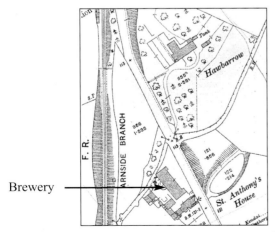

Early 1900's Ordnance Survey showing **Tattersall's Brewery** behind St. Anthony's House and the reservoir on the opposite side of the main road.

Looking north to Heversham from Milnthorpe Hill c.1920. **St. Anthony's House** is on the right, Fairmead and its walled garden are in the middle distance and Parkhouse Farm is on the left.

Tunnel under A6 at St. Anthony's. This connected a small reservoir on the east side of the road with Tattersall's Brewery behind the house on the west. Except for a surviving stone vault, the Heversham Brewery was demolished around 1905 when Tattersall's decided to concentrate on their main brewery in Blackburn.

Fairmead in 1975 when it was my family's home. It was built by Edward Abbot in 1919. Costing the enormous sum for the time of £3,000 it boasted H and C in all bedrooms, fitted wardrobes and central heating plus an acre of garden with a croquet lawn.

The only extant photograph of me engaged in any form of sporting activity –seen here playing **croquet at Fairmead** with my nephew Karl Thurnhill in the hot dry summer of 1976.

Parkhouse Farm in 1920. Currently the home of Gordon and Mary Capstick , it has belonged to the Levens Hall estates since the 16th century and has been tenanted by many renowned farming families including the Websters, Barnes, Dobsons and Bindlosses.

Splendid half cruck beams and rafters in the **barn at Parkhouse Farm** which probably date back to the 15th century when the building could have been the Tithebarn for St. Mary's Abbey at York to which Heversham Church belonged. It is possibly one of the largest medieval barns in the country.

Clipping time at Parkhouse c. 1900. The shearers are sitting on the site of the pre-turnpike road which can be seen behind and which joins the A6 close to the south end of The Prince's Way. The farm track curves off to the left.

Gordon Capstick's home made wagon being driven from Parkhouse Farm passed Plumtree Hall on the way to Leasgill School's centenary celebrations in 1991. 1n 1823 a 'Sale Notice' for Plumtree Hall stated 'there is excellent and convenient sea bathing and several **Stage Coaches** pass the front of the Hall'.

One of Heversham's newest residents one day old **Luke Miles Edmondson** of Parkhouse Farm born on 23 May 2007, with parents Mark and Rachel nee Capstick. Mark's family farm at High Barns another Levens Estate property and their wedding in 2002 was the first anybody could remember occurring between leading tenant families.

A reminder of olden times: Gordon Capstick, with Lenny Mason, driving **a Victorian 'Doctor's Trap'** along the old coaching road through Parkhouse Farm.

Hawbarrow and the A6 c.1910. Hawbarrow was built 'as his summer residence' for Rev. George Marsham Argles, a Canon of York Minster. The site was originally called Hallbarrow Close but the house has been called Howbarrow 1906, Hawbarrow 1910, Horbarrow 1960, Hall Barrow Park 1980 and Hallbarrow 2007. The road got a tarmac surface in 1913 and the telegraph poles, installed in 1851, were only removed in the 1970s.

The white stone by Hawbarrow's entrance drive is the boundary stone inscribed HM dividing the Heversham and Milnthorpe civil parishes. Just in front is the start of Workhouse Lane leading to Ackenthwaite.

Mrs Ellwood in Court Dress. From 1945 to the 1960s she was the **chatelaine of Horncop**. As the step daughter of the Lancaster Lino millionaire Lord Ashton, she was enormously rich and in the 1950s she maintained a full establishment of cook, two maids, full time gardener and a chauffeur. Except when being driven out in her green Rover by her Chauffeur Cecil Starkie she was hardly ever seen.

Even so she was a generous financial supporter of village causes and her £400,000 will (about £10m in the value of 50 years later) included a bequest of £2000 to 'augment the Living of Heversham'.

HORNCOP, HEVERSHAM.

VOTE FOR CURWEN

THE MAN ON THE SPOT.

Colours: RED and WHITE.

Horncop

County election leaflet of 1913 for John Flavel Curwen showing his residence which, being a professional architect, he designed for himself in 1900. The name derives from his former home at Horncop Hall, Kendal. In the early twentieth century **J.F.Curwen** was Westmorland's most prolific, and distinguished, local historian. On his death in 1932 he endowed the Curwen Archives Trust to support local research.

OUR LOCAL EXPRESS
Sandside to Kendal and back in one day, via Heversham

1910 Postcard depicting the less than speedy **Arnside to Hincaster Branch Line.** Granddad Handley of Heversham Hall could remember the opening of the line in 1876 and was still alive when it closed in 1963. The five mile single track was built by the Furness Railway and connected the F.R.'s Carnforth to Barrow line at Arnside with the North West main line at Hincaster Junction. It was designed as a short cut to ease congestion at Carnforth Station for west bound coke trains from the Durham coal field and iron ore and limestone goods trains heading east.

FURNESS RAILWAY

Ellerhow in the mid 1950s showing the branch line with wooden sleepers. They were replaced by concrete sleepers in 1960, only three years before the line was torn up following the Beeching Axe of 1963. The house was designed by Stephen Shaw and built during the Great War for a Kendal pharmacist Christopher Taylor. In 1957 the Fawcett family changed the name of their home to **'Tidal Reaches'** but until a newer property Lawnswood was built in the adjacent paddock locals called it 'the house in the field'.

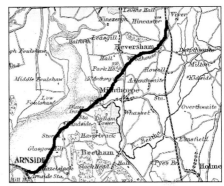

The Arnside to Hincaster Branch Line

Heversham Station operated between 1890 and 1942. Though convenient for Heversham Grammar School Boarders passenger traffic declined when the Dallam Bus service started between local villages and Kendal in 1924. After standing derelict for 20 years the station was cleared away in 1960-but the platform remains.

Pathway from the A6 just north of Heversham Bridge to the Station. As there was no vehicle access passengers requiring help with luggage rang a bell by the roadside gate to attract the porter Tommy Walker.

'Kendal Tommy' ran from Grange to Kendal and was the chief passenger train on the branch line. Here we see 'him' decked out, in 1908, to convey Queen Victoria's fourth daughter Princess Louise, Duchess of Argyle who had been visiting the Bagots at Levens Hall.

Heversham from the air in 1933 showing the Prince's Way to the left and the village street laid down in c.1820. The diagonal south east pointing wall close to Church Farm at the top of the street near the newly built bungalows marks **the line of the original village street** which curved round the site of the Grammar School in the right foreground to meet Parkhouse drive which took the road south to Milnthorpe. Already The Prince's Way's concrete surface of 1927 has been partly replaced and the first houses have been built. Four substantial semis were later built just beyond the trees centre left. A still undeveloped Dugg Hill is shown in the right corner.

The house in the trees in the top right was the Vicarage from 1844 to 1948.

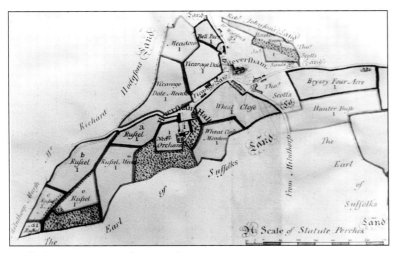

18th Century Map of Heversham showing the original road curving in from the south, the Church and field names.

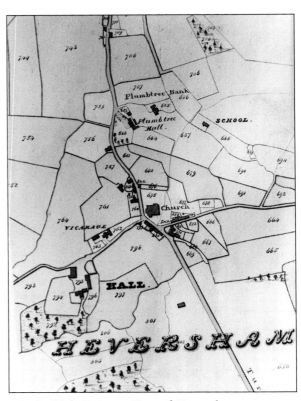

Early 19th Century Map of Heversham showing the newer straighter road which became the village street. The numbers probably refer to the Poor Rate assessment. Number 668 between 667 and 669 clearly shows the track of the old road.

The southern entrance to the village about 1950 with the entrance to **Dugg Hill** on the right.

One of the first houses on **Dugg Hill in 1935**.

View from Heversham Head of **Dugg Hill estate**, begun in 1966. Prices ranged from £2,650 to £4,950 - but the Show House was £6,250.

The Grammar School Entrance in the Village Street, being decorated for the Coronation celebrations of King George V and Queen Mary 1911.

The village street c. 1910 with the Grammar School on the left and Springfield Houses on the right.

37

Two pairs of semis built on the **village street around 1910**. The nearest house 'Fairfield' was the home of the Sedgwick family. **Bannersgate**, the second house on the right was the home of Hubert Simpson the noted Kendal Arts and Crafts Furniture designer and manufacturer.

Church Farm before the house was divided in 1955 to provide separate homes for Nancy Whitwell and her husband John Tyson and, also, for her father Giles and sister Mary Whitwell. The shaded window was the farm dairy. Mr. Cross from next door grew prize winning sweet peas in the front garden. For 49 years until 1980 the Whitwell family ran the Post Office here.

Nancy Whitwell delivering milk to Mrs Sedgwick at Fairfield c. 1935 - before milk bottles came in.

Mary Whitwell who took over from her mother as **P... Mistress** about 1950. Her nephew Martin Tyson still has ... counter in his attic.

Woodhouse Lane showing the former **Eagle and Child Inn** about 1906 shortly after it became a **'Temperance Hotel'**. Later it was the village Social Club which boasted a full sized Billiards Table.

William Noble to whom Colonel Budworth dedicated "A Fortnight's Ramble to the Lakes" 1795. The Colonel described **Happy Times at the Eagle and Child** where the landlady charged only 8d for his dinner.

Close up of **The Eagle and Child signpost** from a 1900 postcard. The railings went to make weapons of war in 1940.

THE fexton was landlord of the Eagle and Child, and, whilft his good woman was dreffing our dinner, we were induced, from feeing a number of boys fhoes, and hearing the found of a fiddle in a barn, to become fpectators. About thirty boys and girls were affembled for a quarter's inftruction. The mafter had more the appearance of a man than that of a dancing-mafter, although he was well qua-

The Colonel on **dancing at Heversham** over 200 years ago.

Woodhouse Lane 1980.

1920s Road sign.

Woodhouse Lane after the former Social Club in the old Eagle and Child had been converted into separate dwellings. The 'Bad Bends' sign (formerly outside The Club) has been transferred to the west wall of Heversham Cottage.

Looking down Woodhouse Lane c. 1950 showing valerian growing in the cobbles in front of Heversham Cottage and the attached barn demolished in the late fifties. It was formerly used as a shippon by Giles Whitwell of Church Farm whose farmyard was opposite. Hincaster folk used to park their bikes in the barn having cycled two miles to catch the bus at Heversham.

Mr and Mrs Dockray with their children Bertha (later Mrs Vaudrey), Edgar and Edith Cassandra in the garden of **Heversham Cottage** shortly after the family came to live here in 1911. The garden was on the other side of the lane from the house and is now the site of Holly Close. Edith's son **Thomas Geoffrey Bibby** (1917-2001) became a famous archaeologist in Denmark and was one of the few natives of Heversham to have merited a full Obituary in The Times.

Cows in the yard of Church Farm.   ..and pigs.

4 and 3 Bay View. Until piped water arrived in the early 1900s there were no houses up Woodhouse Lane east of Heversham Cottage which had the last well on the spring line. 30 detached villas and bungalows were built from 1910 onwards. The Bay View houses were originally **Council Houses** built in 1948 on land compulsorily purchased from the Audland family. No 4 had a tragic early history as just before the Coronation celebrations of 1953 Mary Hallmark, who lived there, died leaving a newborn baby and three small children.

In the garden at **No 3 Bay View c.1957** before the garden wall, on which there was a spectacular Albertine rose, was set back to create a lay-by opposite the grave yard. L to R Kathleen Bell, Susan Bell, Edith Pearson (from no 4) largely hidden by David Pearson and Brian Pearson. The dog's name has been forgotten. Kathleen with her late husband Jack moved into Number 3 when it was first built and, happily, nearly 60 years later she is still there. The Pearsons subsequently emigrated to Rhodesia as Zimbabwe then was. David and Brian later played squash for England, the only brothers to do so. In the background is **High Meadows** built for Mr Milne, a solicitor, during the First World War. It was then the home for Mr & Mrs P.G. Thompson for 50 years. Philip Thompson was the last Chairman of Westmorland County Council. Rex Gyngell who later lived there was a Cumbria County Councillor, and leader of the Conservative Group on CCC.

Whinfell and **The Vicarage, Woodhouse Lane** about 50 years ago. These two large houses were built c.1928, on the site of a wooden chalet bungalow called The Knoll which was built about 1906 and which blew down about 1920. The house on the right was bequeathed to the Church by Mrs Rhoda Thompson in 1948 to be used as a Vicarage. At the time it was considered that this five bedroomed house in half an acre of garden would be a smaller and more convenient house for the Rev and Mrs Cleghorn who, being without a family, could 'manage' with a resident housekeeper, Clara Knight, aided by dailies and a gardener.

Chestnut House c.1900 when it accommodated Sissons Tea Rooms. The house was originally The Ship Inn but became the Grammar School Boarding House. When the new road was built in 1820 the house was set back and given its late Georgian facade. In the 1940s the Grammar School used it, briefly, as a Boarding House again.

Name stone on the house built for my uncle and aunt **Eddie and Audrey Rushton** on Woodhouse Lane 1959. According to the internet it is the only such address in the country. The name is taken from that of the track on to Heversham Head to the west of 'Whinfell'. It refers to the transhumance method of farming whereby stock is regularly shifted (often in a hurry or 'fluster') from wet land 'down't marsh' up to 'hard land' on the hills. In the 1950's Fluster Gap was also on the Grammar School's Fell Race course when it was mistakenly called by the PT (not 'PE') master 'Fosters Gap'. This usage was copied even by local lads in the belief that their parents and grand parents must be wrong in sticking to the old name.

Mashiter's Pantechnicon outside Chestnut House in 1914.

The Great North Road 1924. Soon Heversham was relieved from what was considered to be traffic congestion when The Prince's Way, one of the nation's first by-passes, was opened in 1927.

Son Row. Around 1830 the terraced cottages earned this nickname because all the resident's surnames ended in 'son' being: Wilson, Hanson, Johnson, Hodgson, two Sissons, Gregson, Jenkinson and Nicholson. The white door is that of the village shop.

Signpost at the bottom of Woodhouse Lane in the Village Street showing the **A6 addition** to the sign which after the main road was diverted to The Prince's Way in 1927 was merely painted over.

A rare scene nowadays - **Jean Shuttleworth,** in c.1980, at **the village shop counter** with a huge selection of mix and match behind. From 1962 Jean with her husband Russell ran the shop for 37 years.

Further along the Row c.1900. The cross marks a shop which, until her death, in 1960 was run by **Polly Hoggarth.**

Polly's father Henry Hoggarth. When he died at the age of 96 in 1937 he w Heversham's oldest inhabitant and had 'been out walking the day before'. originally came to the village from Brougham to be the 'hind' or farm man for the Rev. Dr. Hart Headmaster of the Grammar School from 1872-189 Some people can still remember him which is an interesting link with the as **'Old Hoggarth'** was born 167 years ago.

Water colour by Winifred Slater, 1967, showing the old peat sheds at the corner of Son Row and Moss Lane. They were replaced by a detached house in the 1990s. The arch on the right was originally the North entrance to the church and was moved here about 1820. It became the garden gate of the Vicarage which later became The Blue Bell. When The Prince's Way cut the garden in two-the part nearest the Church became the site for Herbert Valentine Killshaw's bungalow and joiners shop.

H. KILSHAW & SON

JOINERS & FUNERAL DIRECTORS, PAINTERS & DECORATORS.

HEVERSHAM - Milnthorpe

CREMATIONS ARRANGED

Telephone: MILNTHORPE 79

Tommy Alan beside the old arch. Tommy worked at the joiner's workshop for 59 years starting as a 14 years old apprentice for Herbert Kilshaw in 1945, then, successively, for Norman Kilshaw until 1976, John Fishwick to 1984, Eric Proctor to 1993 and finally for Bill Gott until he, sort of, retired in 2004.

One of Leven's Hall's traction engines negotiates the Church Corner during The Silver Jubilee Celebrations in 1977. In the background is **Heversham House.**

Miss Marple lookalikes - **the Austin sisters**, 'Auntie Hilda and Auntie Sybil' in their garden at Heversham House which had a charm redolent of the Edwardian gardens of Gertrude Jekyll and Edwin Lutyens. A group of detached houses called 'Heversham Gardens' now occupies most of the grounds. As Heversham's crime rate has always been virtually nil, the two ladies, unlike Agatha Christie's genteel sleuth, never investigated a murder - 'tho they missed nowt!' As they maintained a semblance of domestic staff, they were able to devote their time to driving their grey car called 'Dovey', painting watercolours, doing embroidery, organising all manner of good works and caring for Heversham Church. For Midnight Mass Miss Austin used to put a crystal dish of Christmas roses on the altar. As the vicar in those days celebrated with his back to the congregation they could only be seen by him and by me - the server. But ever since the sight of Chrismas roses jogs my personal 'Memories of Heversham'.

Heversham House. The gables were added to the Georgian house in 1900 when it was the residence of the historically important architect **Hubert Austin**. His daughters Mrs Sybil Stewart and Miss Hilda Austin lived here until 1967. The house was then occupied firstly by French's, a firm building the M6. Later it became a Grammar School Boarding House before becoming a care home. My mother Phyllis Hall died here in 2004, in the bow windowed former upstairs drawing room.

Retirement Party for Rev Edward Radclyffe Ellis, Vicar 1921-1939 in the garden of Heversham House.
L to R from the back, Mrs Drew, Mrs Astley, Mr Nelson, Mrs Nelson, (church organist), Malcolm (Mac) Sisson, Mr Brownson, Dianne Drew, -, Mrs Stewart, -, Miss Austin, -, Mrs Hales?, Mrs Park, -,-,Mrs McLeod nee Argles, Miss Rooks, Mr Squires (Parish Clerk) Mr Herbert Kilshaw.

Outside **the old Blue Bell** late 1940s. **John Tarves** landlord from 1897-1951 stands in the doorway with Frank Dickinson, 'young Pritchard' and John Pritchard on his right. I can just remember the pub's seats made out of barrels and a collection of cacti. Notice, how successive resurfacing has raised the road above the entrance cobbles.

'Old Tarves' having once been in the service of Scottish Noblemen also acted as a part time Butler. Here he presides at the top of the front steps to Levens Hall as Mrs Annette Bagot is being presented with a bouquet while the chief guest the comedian **George Formby** grins at her side.

Looking south between The Blue Bell and Smithy Cottage. The steps to the Old School are on the left. **Smithy Cottage** was also the Post Office which, no doubt accounts for the little girl peering in at the window. **St. Mary's Well** is just south of the boy.

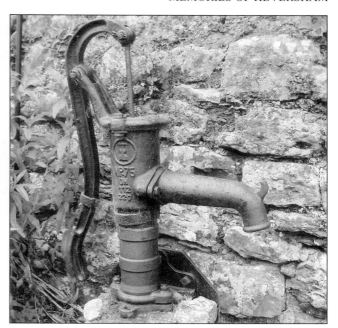

Pump over St. Mary's Well.

ST. MARY'S WELL

The name derives from Ivo de Taillebois' grant of 'Eureshaim' to St Mary's Abbey at York in c.1094. The well provided a public water supply for a thousand years from the time of the Dark Age monastery of 'Hefresham' until piped water arrived in 1908. Around 1900 it was equipped with an Appleby Pump. In 1905 steam haulage vehicles were banned from using its water 'as there was not enough left for village people'. Contamination from the Old School privies allegedly caused 'typhoid to break out amongst the infants' and prompted the school to move to Leasgill in 1891.

The Post Mistress Mrs Varley and her daughter Norah selling flowers and produce outside the **Post Office in 1915.** Norah was awarded the MBE after she became one of the first female Income Tax Inspectors.

Plaque describing St. Mary's well. The inscription was composed by me and the plaque was paid for out of the Leasgill Quarry Fund.

The Blue Bell on the left, Smithy Cottage on the right c.1914. The bay window belonged to the tiny showroom of the **Heversham Metal Work Guild** which was started by Mr P.J. Hibbert in 1891 and continued by his successor at Plumtree Hall Miss Lillian Watson. Metalwork became a remunerative hobby for many villagers until the diversion of passing trade after The Prince's Way was opened led to the showroom being removed in c.1930. But perhaps Arts and Crafts work had gone out of fashion.

Kate and Eileen Hodgson outside Mike and Edith Hodgson's house at **Crow Wood** - opposite the Playground. The four Crow Wood homes, like Bay View, were originally Council Houses built in 1952. Previously the field contained black Galloway Cattle whose trough was filled from water drawn from St. Mary's Well. No one knows where the Crow Wood name came from - although a vociferous colony of rooks occupies the Churchyard conker trees nearby.

Brigadier C. E. Tryon-Wilson, who donated the site next door to the former Blue Bell Inn, swings Andrew and David James at the opening of the **Children's Playing Field** created to celebrate The Silver Jubilee in 1977.

The Golden Jubilee entrance gates for the playground as designed by Tony Parker, who was also Chairman of the Parish Council. They were officially opened by the Brigadier's widow Rosemary Tryon-Wilson of 15th May 2002.

Hooping a wheel. c.1920. At the left John Tarves waits with a watering can to extinguish flames flaring up as the red hot metal rim (the hoop) is being hammered by the smith Harry Varley. The wooden cart wheel is being levered by wheelwright Jim Sisson on the right. The Smithy was across the road from Smithy Cottage.

Lyngarth c.1997.

Advert for the Maltkiln 1823.

A MALT KILN,
With every convenience for carrying on the business of a Maltster, (now in the occupation of Ewan Rawlinson,) in the Village of Heversham, together with a COTTAGE-HOUSE adjoining.

Annbec 2007.

This house was built for Mr and Mrs Ivor Fergusson about 1970 and was rudely nick named the 'fire station' on account of its prominent garage doors and vast area of tarmac. The house was subsequently extended and modified by Ailsa and Michael Hulme who renamed it 'Annbec'. It and the adjoining residence were built in the former kitchen garden of Heversham House. Around 1800 there was a malt kiln and a cottage on the site .

On to Leasgill

Plumtree Hall c. 1908. The house takes its name from an older property Plumtree Bank, just to its east on Heversham Head, which was first recorded as Plummestre in the 16th century. The Hall was built in 1815 for Joseph Braithwaite a former Mayor of Kendal. His descendants the Braithwaite-Wilsons lived here until 1911 when it became the home of the Watson family. For the last thirty years a private trust has provided sheltered accommodation here mainly for older local people 'who have gone into Plumtree'.

Garden entrance at Plumtree Hall. This building was originally a porch added to the old Grammar School on Heversham Head c. 1840. It was transferred to Plumtree when the school moved to the village street in the 1870s.

A 1907 De Dion Bouton drawn up on the drive at Plumtree Hall.

A carriage awaits at the front door.

The carriage and motor car pictures probably date from before 1913 when Mr P.J. Hibbert rented Plumtree but this photo is definitely of the more up to date **Mr and Mrs Bowman Watson** in 1913. They were still going strong in the 1950s.

1823 Advertisement for 'Plumb-Tree Hall'. The Kent Estuary had become a summertime resort and until the 1950s remained 'Westmorland's Little Blackpool' - at least during good weather. Four mail and six stage coaches ran through the village in the 1820s.

LOT I.

All that well and Modern-built Mansion, called

PLUMB-TREE HALL,

Situate in the Village of Heversham, near Milnthorpe, in the County of Westmorland.

This Mansion and Premises consist of a good and pleasantly situated House, with a spacious Hall or Lobby; two large Parlours to the front; House-keeper's Room; Servants' Hall; large Kitchen, Dairy, Brew-house, and every useful and suitable convenience on the ground floor, over which are seven good Bed Rooms, Drawing Room, and a large Room over the Kitchen. There are also spacious WINE and ALE VAULTS. The Out-houses consist of ONE LARGE STABLE with HAY-LOFT; TWO COACH HOUSES; SHIP-PON, HAY-LOFT, &c. &c.

In the front of the Hall is a Lawn, surrounded with choice Fruit and Forest Trees; there is also a Garden and Orchard adjoining it, in the whole containing about an Acre and a half of Land, Statute Measure.

Plumb-Tree Hall is situated on the Kendal and Lancaster Road, is distant from Kendal, six miles; from Bowness (THE LAKE OF WINDERMERE) thirteen; from Lancaster, fifteen; and from the Market Town of Milnthorpe, about one mile, within a mile of which Town there is excellent and convenient

SEA BATHING.

There are several Stage Coaches, and the Mails pass the front of the Hall, within one hundred yards, daily.

Heversham's **'Coronation Procession'** approaches Plumtree from Leasgill in 1911. The road and the pavement have now been tarmaced - but the dressed limestone wall on the right is unchanged.

umtree Bank c. 1985 showing modernisations ...ried out for Mr. and Mrs Bob Parratt to the right ...d house and the 1930s flat roofed extension to Bill ...wson's house left. Bill who was the gardener at ...mtree lived here for over 60 years before retiring ...wn the path into sheltered housing in the Hall ...ere he lived to be 94. The Parratts then moved into ...l's house. From 1613 to about 1820 Plumtree Bank ...s the residence of the Grammar School 'Master'.

Park's Victory Row c. 1905 acquired its name as it was built at the time of the British triumph over Napoleon in 1815. Here we see 16 members of the Metcalf, Proctor, Sisson and Strickland families who somehow crammed themselves into the four two bedroomed cottages.

Looking up the road also in the 1900s. Just in front of the steps was a workshop later converted into Heversham's first garage and petrol station where Sergeant Park also charged wireless accumulator batteries. Opposite are Strickland House, Rose Cottage and, facing south, Yew Tree House all of which were built on the former track of the original road which accounts for all the properties occupying narrow sites.

Leasgill showing the old 'low road' on the left with the 1820 Turnpike Road on the right. Long View cottages on the top right date from around 1840. The cast iron white mile 'stone', dated 1826, right foreground was buried during the Second World War to confuse the Wermacht. I can remember seeing its being uncovered, as with my fellow pupils, I toddled back to Leasgill School from the Shrove Tuesday church service in 1947.

Close up of **Rose Cottage** decorated for the 1911 Coronation with, it is thought, the Pattinson brothers outside. The door has since been moved to the right and Rose Cottage like its namesakes further along the road and at Woodhouse lacks a rose.

Applegarth built on the Quarry site in 1996.

Then and Now. The then photo left shows **Sissons joiners shop** which was here for over 100 years before it was replaced by housing in 1996. The site, officially called **Leasgill Quarry**, was parish land having been a common gravel pit. I started a big row when I informed Heversham that under the terms of the separation of Heversham and Milnthorpe in 1896 joint assets if sold had to be divided between the townships with two thirds going to Milnthorpe. After much debate my historical view was found to be legally correct. The upshot was the formation of a trust which amicably shares out the income of about £3,000 pa so that as far as possible both parishes benefit equally.

HEVERSHAM SCHOOL

My 'alma mater' : **Heversham Church of England School** shortly after it moved to Leasgill in 1891 with the boys almost camouflaged amongst the ivy on the Vicarage wall. It is just behind Longview Cottages. In the 1940s their earth privies backed on to the school lane. I attended **Leasgill School** from the 21st October 1946 to 27th July 1954.

Another view of the 1911 gathering with **Highfield** built for the Germaine family c.1900 in the background. Two other houses, Underwood and Leasgill Brow, were erected to the right at about the same time. In the 1940s Leasgill Brow was the home of the Binyons who were relatives of **Laurence Binyon** author of the Remembrance Sunday refrain 'They shall not grow old as we that are left grow old...', said to be the most quoted lines of poetry in the English language.

low road seen in this photo of the **1911 'Coronation Procession'.** Laundry age on the right, was the home of the Parish Mangle which was on the first r approached by steps at the side of the house. Water was collected in a still iving –though now empty-sunken tank which was also used for steam wagons.

'Leasgill Brow' shortly after the house was built in c.1908 when it was called 'Fern Bank'. The subsequent growth of the saplings has completely embowered the house so that it cannot be seen from the road and has provided the name of 'Woodlands Hall' for another residence built to the right of the gate in c.1970.

High Leasgyll c. 1996. A rare, snowy scene in our temperate climate which I often condemn as being "no snow in winter and no sun in summer". This fine house was the **Vicarage** from 1844 until 1948. It was built for the Rev Robert Wilson Evans after the Surveyor Miles Thompson decreed that the original vicarage (which in the 20th century became the Blue Bell Hotel) was 'quite unfit for the Residence of the Incumbent of Heversham'. The new house was designed by Mr. Thompson's partner George Webster and cost £2,600. Its accommodation included a palatial drawing room, dining room, study, kitchen, butler's pantry, housekeeper's room, a cavernous wash house, six principle bedrooms, three servant's rooms, two staircases, wine and beer cellars, a dairy, stable, coach house, shippon, two water closets for the family and an earth closet for the staff. Curiously **no children have ever lived here** as all the Vicars were childless between 1866 and 1955 and the Drew family who moved in, in 1948 , were all grown up as were the family of Mr and Mrs Etheridge who followed the Drews in 1992.

Leasgill Athenaeum c.1970. Heversham must be the only place to have a village hall called The Athenaeum, not that every one can spell it. It occupies an eighteenth century barn given to the village by the Argles family in the 1870s and is named after Mr. Argles' club the Liverpool Athenaeum and not after the clerical London establishment. Over the years it has been regularly modified so that the entrance has moved round the building four times, the first being into the main hall from the road, the next in 1928 a little higher up the road, then on the north side in the 1970s and more recently from the car park on the south side.

Athenaeum sign carved by Parkin and Jackson c. 1985.

Looking south with **Sands Cottage** on the right c.1920. Lilly Taylor kept a shop here in the 1920's and 1930's.

The north side of Leasgill Brow 1904 showing the old road coming in on the left. 80 years earlier it took over a year to dig through the Brow to create the Turnpike which was not completed all the way to Milnthorpe until 1824. The building left background marked with a cross is Sands Cottage long the home of one of the many branches of the Proctor family. The tree said to be a Plane tree gives its name to a cottage just out of the frame.

Audrey Proctor with four smaller children L to R Irene Nelson, Terry Proctor, Dorothy Nelson, Margaret Nelson. The Nelson's father, Gordon, lived to be 99 years 11 months. Behind on the left is **Birdcage Cottage** - which probably got it's name from a cage like grill over the cellar window. In the 1840s John Reed, a former HGS master, used the premises for a short lived and minuscule school - 'good accommodation for four boarders'. **Rose Cottage** on the right was the Nelson's home for 60 years. Gordon grew magnificent chrysanthemums but, as with Heversham's other two Rose Cottages, I cannot remember any roses.

Clark's carriers of Milnthorpe outside Eversley Barn, Leasgill c.1890.

Eversley House c. 1920. It was built in an Italianate style made popular by Queen Victoria's contemporary Osborne House in the mid 1850s for **Frank Atkinson Argles**. On the death of Tom Argles in 1924 the house and much of Leasgill was sold to the Drew family who owned the house until they moved to the former vicarage at High Leasgyll in 1948. Eversley was later divided into four still substantial residences.

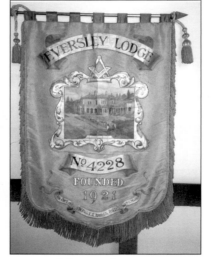

Banner of the Eversley Free Masons' Lodge, Kendal, presented by Thomas Atkinson Argles of Eversley in 1921, showing the south front of his house. The Argles residence also gave its name to the Eversley Choral union. It is understood that there are now other lodges in the area including the Heversham Lodge, one of whose founders was the Rev Tom Martin, Vicar of Heversham 1966-75.

This **sign in the Lay-By** opposite the entrance drive to Eversley is a reminder of Local Government prior to 'reorganisation' in 1974 when the Rural District was absorbed into South Lakeland District Council and Westmorland became part of Cumbria. All the old county signs disappeared overnight on 1st April 1974 only to re-emerge as decoration in private property but, almost uniquely, this **SWRDC sign** has remained in place.

Grievegate c.1965, designed by Mawsons, was built on the site of the Eversley greenhouses in the early 1960s for Dr Patrick Byrne and his wife Dr Kathleen Pearson both of whom were well known local G.P.s. Patrick later became Britain's first Professor of General Practice at Manchester University. Having first met at Liverpool University in the 1930s my parents, at various times, also worked with them at Stoneleigh Surgery, Milnthorpe. 'Uncle Pat' died aged 66 in 1980 but happily in 2007 'Auntie Kathleen', at 94, is still with us. Grievegate takes its name from the old coach road that connected the main road near Levens Bridge with Mabbin Hall Lane.

The **Tollgate House** on the A6 near Levens Hall. Erected around 1800 it was removed when The Princes Way was built. Behind is the garden wall of Levens Hall which, like Milnthorpe Hill over two miles to the south, is within Heversham's ecclesiastical parish.

Levens Bridge 2007.

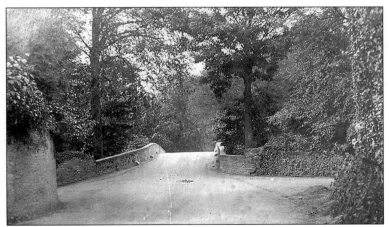

Levens Bridge 1900. Looking south into Heversham.

The Princes Way

The Prince of Wales later Edward VIII and subsequently Duke of Windsor after whom Heversham's bypass, The Prince's Way is named. He is wearing his British Legion Badge as the chief object of his Westmorland Tour of July 1927 was to review ex-servicemen-all of whom said that he was drunk. Even the Westmorland Gazette reported that the 'Prince looked tired and nervously fingered the rim of his bowler'.

HEVERSHAM	.. arrive 6-35 p.m.
	The Lord Lieutenant will present the Chairman of the County Council.
	The Chairman of the County Council wil. present the members of the Councill
	The Chairman of the Main Roads Committee will present to His Royal Highness a pair of gold scissors to cut the tape and ask him to declare the Road open.
	His Royal Highness opens the Road.
	depart 6-45 p.m. via Milnthorpe.

The Prince's brief Heversham itinery. In fact he was late having made an unscheduled stop for a few minutes at Levens Hall which folk memory attributed to HRH's 'tired and nervous state'.

The Prince cuts the ribbon to open the road. On the left is possibly J.F. Curwen, Chairman of Heversham Parish Council. G.H. Pattinson, Chairman of Westmorland County Council is on the right. Councillor Pattinson had earlier insisted that the roadside trees by Levens Hall should be preserved in a central verge thereby creating what is claimed to be the first dual carriage way on the A6.

Building the road. Workmen have just broken through the field walls at the southern end and are laying a light railway.

The same spot today.

The **southern approach** road is almost finished.

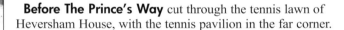

Before The Prince's Way cut through the tennis lawn of Heversham House, with the tennis pavilion in the far corner.

The **northern end** also nearing completion - but the Tollgate House top left has not yet been demolished.

The **tennis pavilion** of Heversham House (above right) was transferred to the courts on Heversham Head and can be seen behind the players c.1940. Nancy Whitwell is on the extreme right.

Roughly the same view showing the road almost completed.

Traffic pounds along **the concrete road** at possibly 40mph c 1930. In the right background is **Frank Varley's filling station.** Younger people were fascinated by Frank's lacking one arm and one leg. We all thought he had 'lost them in the war' but they had been amputated as a result of TB.

A close up of **'Frank's Garage'**. L to R. James Thompson, Frank, Mr Booth, Mac Sisson, Harold East and Mrs Varley. Harold worked for Mr Astley at Greenside, Hincaster, being one of several professional chauffeurs employed around Heversham.

Spout House seen here in c.1930 is the oldest building on The Prince's Way. The Royal Commission on Ancient Monuments in 1936 said that it possessed an 'original window with a solid frame' which was probably 16th century.

Bert Wilson lived at Spout House during the 1940s and 50s. He was a former Millwall and Wigan professional footballer and subsequently the Grammar School's caretaker for 26 years.

k Farm about half way long The Prince's Way lost some of
uildings when the road was made. The hill behind is a
nlin called **Haysteads**. In November 1947 a bonfire was built
he right of the hedge on the top) by Miss Drew with the help
couts and Guides, to celebrate **Princess Elizabeth's Wedding**.
because of incessant rain it was not lit for a fortnight.

Bank Farm was rebuilt in the 1980s after part of the building
fell down while it was being repaired.

1954 advert.

The Heversham Hotel c. 1930's. The chief victim of The Prince's Way
was a private house Elm Lawn, as the road cut its garden in two and came
close to its drawing room windows. Having been the Vicarage until 1842
it now became the unlicensed Heversham Hotel. It only obtained a full
liquor license when the old Blue Bell closed in 1952. The Chew family
changed the establishment's name to The Blue Bell at Heversham in
1966. Such was its reputation that at Jack Chew's funeral in 1977 the vicar
began his address by saying 'when I was first offered the benefice of
Heversham I asked: "Is that where The Blue Bell is?"'.

**The Heversham Hotel's
Festive Menu** when a
French/ Swiss gentleman
Eugene Mabillard was
chef/ proprietor. Included
in the six courses was a
substantial cold buffet to
help fill any gaps-all for
25 shillings-which in real
terms is about the same as
the £45 banquet tariff half
a century later.

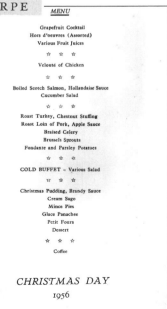

61

Wireless Broadcast from the lounge of The Heversham Hotel, November 1951. Taking part in the **BBC 'Country Magazine'** L to R Jo Cookson, Headmaster of Milnthorpe Primary School, Ralph Wightman - radio 'personality' and writer later much parodied for his regular response- "I think the answer lies in the soil", Miss Kelly, County Girl Guides organiser, Mr. E. Ellis, farmer from Lanefoot, Kendal, Mr A. Hayton, Windermere boatbuilder, Jonty Wilson, Kirkby Lonsdale blacksmith and W. Parkin, huntsman to Lunesdale foxhounds. The nationwide live broadcast was meticulously scripted which resulted in a wooden delivery from participants except from Jo who roared as if he was addressing his school assembly on a good day.

A main stay of the Blue Bell for 40 years, restaurant manager-Sheila Healey –**'Irish Sheila'** or 'have a bon (bun) Sheila' with Barman Keith Redhead.

Gladys Benson neé James was a local lady who served at the Blue Bell for even longer than Sheila.

Licensee / Proprietor **John Chew** watering The Princes Way verge-drought summer 1976 when ties were still compulsory for restaurant patrons a well as for the boss. As John Chew demonstrated in 1976 we never have a hose pipe ban.

In 2002 the Blue Bell made a welcoming venue for the **Golden Jubilee Celebrations** despite Heversham's over typical summer weather.

Bridie Hewitt, a waitress who had just won the **Miss Lunesdale title**, being pushed in a wheelbarrow by gardener Jimmy Freer with barmaid Julie Cronin looking on c. 1960. The greenhouse which contained a prolifically fruiting vine and a peach tree had survived from the days when the Misses Woods lived here when the house was called Elm Lawn.

4: Farming, Farmhouses and Farming Folk

Heversham's settlement pattern is typical of the area as apart from the village itself, most of which was built in the 20th century, and its straggling off shoot of Leasgill there are several other smaller groupings of hamlets and farms including Hincaster, Woodhouse, Deepthwaite, Rowell and Haverflatts.

Heversham Hall in c.1910. Although within sight and sound of the Church Clock the Hall is cut off from the village by The Prince's Way and is set back from the Marsh Lane beyond the Blue Bell Hotel. The Handley family have farmed here since 1877 as tenants of the squires of the Dallam Tower estate whose ancestor Edward Wilson bought the property from Jasper Buskell in 1614. Until the Dissolution of the Monasteries in the 1530s the Hall had belonged to St. Mary's Abbey at York.

View of the Church c.1840 showing the original gates (removed to the Churchyard's west entrance in 1894) and the famous chestnut trees which traditionally were planted by the Rev. Dr. George Lawson, Vicar from 1797-1842.

Products of the Heversham Metalwork Guild made between 1891 and 1928. (see also p48)

Parable of the Sower.

Parable of the Wise and Foolish Virgins.

Memorial Windows in the south aisle in the church to Robert Wilson Evans Vicar of Heversham 1841 - 66 and who was also the first Archdeacon of Westmorland. They were designed by the renowned Victorian firm Clayton & Bell who were currently working on the windows for the Albert Memorial Chapel at Windsor.

Exquisitely embroidered **banner by Jean Sowerby** 199

Piped band leading the newly married managers of The Blue Bell, Susan and Richard Cowie in 1997. The village store and Post Office closed in 2005.

Leasgill c.1910. (see page 52)

Heversham Grammar School, Sports Day 11th May 1957 Watercolour by R. K. Bingham.

A drizzly **Children's Sports Day at Leasgill, 1970s.** My mother, Phyllis Hall, as one of the Fancy Dress judges, cranes forward between the British Grenadier, Neil ? Shaw and Worzel Gummidge, next comes James Smith with Mortar Board, Andrew Douthwaite in a dustbin, a brolly man and a rude labrador with Alan Casey.

Spring
A Wordsworthian host at Eversley
1990 showing the northern half of
the mansion at that time the home
of Roger and Marjorie Whittaker.

Summer
Combine on the 'Wire Fence
Field' Heversham Marsh 1985
with Dallam Park in the left
background and Haverbrack to
the right.

Autumn
Farmers Glory - Tatie Picking
Moss Side Farm 1985. L to R
Ivor Westmorland, Brian
Atkinson, Andrew Walkden,
Arthur Riley, Michael Barnes.

Winter on the Marsh.
Teal on the northern stretch of the
Kent Estuary. Oil - Peter Scott
1957. (Copyright Whitby and Co.,
Kendal). The famous painter,
ornithologist, author, broadcaster
and wildfowler was regularly
seen around Heversham while on
his many visits to the Kent
Estuary.

Watercolour of School Cottage c.1880 showing the mistress's washing hanging out to to dry.

Heversham Hall Farm, Watercolour by Sybil Stewart c.1940.

The Kent Estuary looking towards Hallforth and Whitbarrow Scar.
Mixed Media - Margaret Evans Fisher 2007.

Watercolour by Howard Somervell 1930 of view from Heversham Head across the Kent's meander at Halforth - known because of its earlike shape as **'the lug'** - with Whitbarrow Scar in the background.

Heversham's Millennium **Beating the Parish Bounds** walk-in May 2000. Chris Baines followed by Roger Whittaker stride/plod over the sea banking. Peter Shaw, the Parish Clerk, and John Chew are just over Roger's shoulder.

Bobby Handley shearing a tup 'bought at Stirzaker's sale, April 1988'. Bobby and his wife Jean farmed **College Green**, 'out on't marsh'. It takes its name from Trinity College Cambridge which was endowed with some of Heversham's former church land by Queen Mary Tudor in 1556.

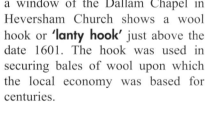

Jasper Buskell's coat of arms from a window of the Dallam Chapel in Heversham Church shows a wool hook or **'lanty hook'** just above the date 1601. The hook was used in securing bales of wool upon which the local economy was based for centuries.

A group of local **children and evacuees admire lambs** in the Hall meadow, 1940. L to R Shirley Henderson, Nelly Hamer, ?, Marj Huntherson, ?, Joan Handcock.

Heversham Hall orchard. George Handley who with his wife, another Jean Handley, currently occupies the Hall photographed in 1996 with his brother, another John Handley, and Roger Bingham. George had just demanded a farthing payment from me after I had casually plucked a damson off the tree. The debt has neither been acknowledged nor paid and George is now claiming interest.

Ruin at the back of the Hall always, but probably inaccurately, known as the **Pele Tower** c.1930.

Georgie aged four **and 'Nip'** or he might be 'Bonzo'.

The Court Room in the Hall showing 14th century windows, part of the wide fireplace and the **Elizabethan table**. J. F. Curwen noted in 1930 'the top which sits loosely upon a massive frame is one solid plank of heart of oak, some five inches thick and measuring 13 feet 8 inches in length, by 2 feet 9 inches in width'. Manorial courts and the Council of 24 men, which ran the Parish until parish councils started in the 1890s, met here.

Greenhead Farm, Hincaster, in c.1970. Greenhead was the first farm worked by the Handleys in the parish.

John Handley, son of William Handley of Greenhead, won a special **Centenary Medal** at the 1899 County Show for the best male shorthorn 'Lord Douglass'.

William Handley's shorthorn bull **'Pearl King'** champion in the 'Aged Bull' class at the Westmorland County Show in 1888. William won international renown with his shorthorns. Once, he sold a beast for £3,000 to a South American dealer.

Inmans's Friesians, the breed which took over from Shorthorns.

Dad and his Lad. Mike Inman with son David at
Milton Moor Farm c.1970.

Mr T. Sanderson of Woodlands Nurseries, (opposite Milton Moor) in
1951 with his **Swedish Landrace Boar** with whom - or with which -
he intended to 'establish this famous breed of bacon pig in
Westmorland'.

Champion Friesian Bull belonging to Rolly Mason
from Lower Rowell Farm c 1960.

Lower Rowell Farm is one of Heversham's oldest buildings. The Royal Commission for Ancient Monuments of 1936 states that it "was built probably early in the 16th century ... the main doorway is original and has moulded jambs and depressed arch in a square head with a moulded label; above the doorway is a panel with initials and date R.P. 1719 (for Rowland Parker)".

Roly-who never wore a cap-Mason takes a break from agriculture's arduous toil at Lower Rowell c.1950.

Close up of **date stone installed 150 - 200 years after the house was built.**

Lower Haverflatts

1987. Mrs Dowker prepares milk for the calves. No longer a farmhouse the property was much altered when converted into several homes in the 1990s. Fortunately the porch datestone 1691 survived.

Haverflatts had some land on the marsh seen below during harvesting in the late 1950s. **Haver** comes from the Viking word for bread or for oats which was always the area's main cereal. The same word also gives us the word 'haversack'-bread bag.

Bernard Dowker shearing sheep at Haverflatts also in the 1950s.

Champion Young Farmer Neil Dowker in **Hedging** Competition. 30 years on Neil in 2007 is YFC's Southern Cumbrian District President.

Sadly the Dowkers no longer live at Haverflatts, though Neil Dowker farms some of its land. The **'bottom dairy'** seen in this photo of Bernard with granddaughter Laura is now called **'Thistledown Cottage'**.

MILNTHORPE, WESTMORLAND.

Particulars and Plan

OF A VALUABLE CUSTOMARYHOLD AND

FREEHOLD ESTATE,

CALLED

LOWER HAVERFLATTS,

SITUATE NEAR

MILNTHORPE, IN THE COUNTY OF WESTMORLAND,

COMPRISING A

DWELLING HOUSE, BARN, STABLE,

SHIPPON, & OTHER CONVENIENT FARM BUILDINGS,

AND

SEVERAL CLOSES OR PARCELS OF EXCELLENT

ARABLE, MEADOW, AND PASTURE LANDS,

CONTAINING TOGETHER

49a. 1r. 34p.,

Like many other properties Lower Haverflatts has changed its address slightly. This **1876 Sale Poster** refers to the current Higher Haverflatts.

Map of the property showing the farms marked as **Haverflatts and Lower Haverflatts**. The Squire family who sold Haverflatts went to live at Leasgill Lodge where Bobby Squire remained until his death in 1946.

Bobby Squire at snowdrop time in the garden of Leasgill Lodge photographed by his Godson Mac Sisson to whom he left the house. This photograph now hangs in the Church Vestry to commemorate Mr. Squires' 40 years service as Parish Clerk from 1906-1946.

Higher Haverflatts (i.e. the former Lower Haverflatts) as rebuilt by its new landlord the brewer William Tattersall in 1882. When this photo was taken in 1987 the Burch family farmed here.

Higher Haverflatts in the 1990s when the farm buildings were being converted into dwellings.

oodhouse 50 years ago. Until c.1800 most of this area s a common called **Woodhouse Green**. The main house s built by Samuel Taylor Haslam in 1856 but it corporates part of an Elizabethan window from an earlier velling. Behind is **High House** which between 1792 and 27 was part of the **Woodhouse Charity Estate** queathed to the Heversham Church Wardens by Nancy eston to provide alms for the poor.

Most farmhouses have been rebuilt many times. Here we see **Woodhouse Farm** c. 1907. Before Woodhouse Green was enclosed the road to Hincaster probably ran between the barn and the house.

Woodhouse Farm today-showing how it was altered by the Johnson family c.1914. With his wife Diane, Woodhouse is farmed by Brian Barnes a member of another long established family. Unlike many of their former dairying neighbours the Barnes 'still milk but maybe not for much longer'.

The **16th century window** at Woodhouse.

Haverwood, opposite Woodhouse Farm, was an award winning development designed by Ashworths and built by Rockcliffe Brothers in 1969. Here we see Colin and Hilary James' son Andrew tottering across the building site. Their house cost £6,150, three times Colin's salary as the Grammar School's head of science. The asking price in 2007 would be £300,000 or eight times a senior teacher's salary.

Ralph Cummings muck spreading by hand - or rather by fork, Greenside, Hincaster c. 1940.

Builder **Frank Rockcliffe** also farmed **High Cragg Yeat**, Ackenthwaite which is also in the ecclesiastical parish. Here we see him haymaking with his brother Keith on the left in c. 1960.

Wartime 'tatie' picking on the Marsh. The men are a German Prisoner of War Franz Smitch, Tom Park and Peter Handley. The ladies are **'Land Girls'**.

There are more snaps of haytime than of any other farming activity perhaps because early cameras required lots of natural light and you cannot make hay unless the sun shines. But this scene captured by Hubert Simpson showing **John Handley mowing hay in 1930** is of better quality. Clara Knight is the figure on the far side of The Prince's Way. Sadly the fine sycamore having become dangerous was cut down to a stump in 2007 - but it is beginning to sprout again.

Loading Hay in the Hall Meadow with L to R Dick Nicholson, Matthew Watson and 'Young' Dimmock, 1930s.

Jenny Sisson, Granddad Sisson in the foreground and the rest of the family **turning hay at Leasgill** in the field on which the Bowling Green was later laid out.

Jim Barnes on top of the **straw cart Moss Side** 1950s. The other figures are Bob and Pat –but contrary to the usual nomenclature Bob is the Irish labourer while Pat is the canine supervisor.

If not stored safely hay can combust resulting in barn fires. Here we see the **burnt out ruins at Ninezergh** in August 1915.

Ninezergh 1906. William Bennet second left, Mrs Bennet sweeping up, young Bill Bennet on horse back plus farm staff. A hundred years ago it was said that 'farm sarvants wer alus that hungered down't Ninezergh' that they used to cook eggs filched from farm yard hens and cook them in the fields.

Ploughing on the Marsh c.1900.

Ploughing on the marsh 1987 - Mike Barnes in the cab.

Erecting a banner during the **Foot and Mouth crisis, Autumn 1967.** As in the outbreak in 2001 such warnings perhaps contributed to the plague's bypassing Heversham. On the right are some of the trees spared in 1928 following Councillor G.H. Pattinson's suggestion that a duel carriageway should be created. (See page 58) Just off the picture beyond the Levens Hall gardens (to the left) is the lane to Ninezergh Farm where in both crises Jim and Helen Bland successfully kept visitors and the dreaded infection at bay.

Tom and Chris Inman **ploughing at Milton Moor** 1930s.

Left: 16 men on hand for **Threshing Day, Heversham Hall c.1914**, Down to the 1950s news 'that thrashers coming' was considered a valid excuse for farmers' children to be absent from Leasgill School.

Modern times down at Halforth - on Nelson's **silage tip** in 2005.

Indoor and outside **staff at Kidside**, near Milton Moor early 1900s.

Starting them young. Billy Strickland learning to clean up at Eversley Farm, or Croft's Farm, early 1930s.

Richard and Bruce Nelson take a **ride on a Suffolk tup** c. 1970.

Happy times for the Barnes family, Moss Side, summer 1979. L to R Tony, pony Magic, Maureen and pet lambs Tom and Tilly. Maureen recalls 'Magic adopted the pet lambs and did not like people going in the field or even other sheep coming near them. She was like a sheep dog and rounded them up if they mixed with anything or anybody'.

'Johnny Pick' feeding sheep in his best clothes.

Throughout the 20th century **Young Farmers Clubs** provided a pivotal educational and social experience for rural youth –and a marriage market. Heversham's branch was the **Kent Estuary YFC**. In 1952 three Kent Estuary members won the Westmorland Gazette Cattle Shield for stock judging. L to R Tony Gibson, John and Robin Pickthall. Tony later farmed Ninezergh and then Beetham Hall, John perpetuated his family's dynasty at Bradley Farm, Hincaster, while Robin went to Lane Farm, Milton Moor before taking a larger spot in north Cumbria. Sadly, all three died relatively young.

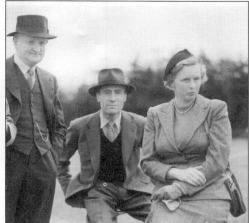

Wearing a watch chain and 'weskit' George Pickthall, surveys **a rural 'do'** with **Westmorland's M.P. Colonel William Vane** and Mrs Vane 'who doesn't look best pleased'.

Bradley Farm, Hincaster c. 1970 home of the Pickthalls since 1894. John's wife Dr Daphne Low, missing her native Australian sunshine, had the yews cut down because 'they made her parlour dark'.

The Date Stone at Bradley Farm refers to an extension made by the Barker family who owned the property until it was purchased by John and Daphne Pickthall. Inside, is some older oak panelling and a splendid 1930's Aga, still in continuous use.

Some of the **latest generation of the Pickthalls** of Bradley Farm, Hincaster, sitting on an archaeological relic, photographed in bright sunshine on St. Swithin's Day 2007. L to R Bernard, Jessica, Karen and Madeline. The 'relic' is a **'milk stand'** on which aluminium 'milk kits' were manhandled for collection by the 'milk wagon' which took them to Libby's 'Milk Factory' at Ackenthwaite from c.1934 until 'Milk Tankers' came in during the 1970's. Unlike some milk stands this one has not been listed as 'an ancient monument' - yet.

Sunnyside, Woodhouse Lane mid 1950s. Formerly called Lane Cottage this property was an ancient small holding recorded on a 17th century Levens Hall estate map. Since 1967 it has been the home of Bill and Anita Gott who have doubled its size and purchased the surrounding fields. A famous Dahlia grower Bill has made full use of the well cultivated garden seen here.

Greenside House, Hincaster. Some of our farmhouses like Heversham and Hincaster Halls were originally Manor Houses. Other farmhouses, like Greenside rebuilt for Thomas Rogers in 1880 became mansions more or less divorced from the land. From c.1930 to 1954 Frederic Astley and family lived here along with a domestic staff which included a chauffeur who lived in the Lodge. I recall going to a children's party at Greenside where I expected to see the chauffeur's children - but they weren't invited. But to my mortification, they waved from the Lodge garden, as we drove up the drive.

Deepthwaite House c. 1991, before it was converted into several dwellings which changed the historic appearance of the centuries old farmhouse. In the early 1800s **William Whewell** boarded here with the Bindloss family when he attended Heversham Grammar School before he headed for Cambridge and, ultimately, international fame as the philosopher who coined the word **'scientist'**.

Date Stone on Greenside Stables. The stables had hot and cold running water laid on for the horses. The Chauffeur's family at the Lodge did not have H and C and 'had to make do with a tin bath'.

Deepthwaite Farm, Bridge and Stainton Beck c.1954. The bridge is listed in the RHCM record as being Elizabethan while a recently discovered wooden mullion window indicates that the house may be at least as old. The name Deepthwaite illustrates **the settlement pattern of the area**. 'Thwaite' comes from the Old Norse Viking word meaning a clearing in the woods. 'Deep' might simply refer to the 'Beck' which like other names for a stream such as 'Gill' and 'Syke' is also of Scandinavian origin. So too, are 'Moss' for Marsh, 'Tarn' and 'Mere' for a lake, 'Scar' for a cliff and 'Shippon' for a cow shed or milking parlour. Heversham's name comes from the Anglo-Saxon 'ham' for a settlement. The 'Hever' part might derive from a personal name 'Haefar' or from 'Eofor' meaning a wild pig. As Deepthwaite is a mile from Heversham village it would seem that the **Viking off-comers** settled down close to, but apart from, the host community. Similarly the original norse settlement of Ackenthwaite is a mile or so from the original 'danish' village of Milnthorpe-which lies in between the Anglo-Saxon homes ('hams') of Beetham and Heversham.

L.5821. Hollycroft Deepthwaite Milnthorpe.

Hollycroft, Deepthwaite c.1910. This imposing Edwardian Villa was built by Thomas Marshall 'Supervisor of Inland Revenue' for Kendal in 1908/9 on Barn Close, part of Deepthwaite Farm which he had purchased for £2,570 in 1906. As well as the family group in the foreground a veiled ghostlike figure may be diserned looking through the conservatory window. Like other properties in the parish 'Hollycroft' has had several name changes being called 'Deepthwaite Lodge' by F.P. Heath in 1930, 'Willow Brae' by Mr and Mrs Gardener in the 1950s until the 1970s when Peter and Talia Johnson re-christened their home 'Keldrigg House' which their successors, the Dootsons, shortened to **'Keldrigg'.**

84

5: Schools

Edward Wilson-who founded Heversham Grammar School for the promotion of 'Godliness and good learning' in **1613**.

The 1613 date carved on the lintel to Big School, came from the old Grammar School on Heversham Head.

The Wilson's flaming crescent crest carved on a pew in the Dallam Chapel in Heversham Church. Although Edward Wilson had no children of his own he also founded the fortunes of the Wilsons of Dallam Tower who still hold much land in Heversham and Milnthorpe. The local Comprehensive formed by the merging of HGS and Milnthorpe Secondary Modern School took the name of **Dallam School in 1984**.

HGS Commemorative plaque is in Big School, now part of the 'Heversham Campus' of Dallam School. In 2007 Dallam is Cumbria's last split site secondary school. Hopefully when remaining activities are removed to the main Milnthorpe site this and other reminders of HGS will be retained.

HEVERSHAM SCHOOL

1613 FOUNDED 1613 HEVERSHAM SCHOOL 1984

The semi derelict **old Grammar School c.1910** on Heversham Head about 40 years after the school moved down the hill to the village.

Richard Watson, Bishop of Llandaff. He was the son of Rev Thomas Watson, Master from 1698-1737.
He was a Chemistry Professor, Vice-President of the Board of Agriculture, a principal founder of the Westmorland County Show and was reputed, inaccurately, never to have visited his Diocese.

William Whewell (1794-1866) might be considered to be HGS's most distinguished scholar. He became Master of Trinity College, Cambridge and gave his name to Whewell Court where he coined the word **scientist**.
Whewell's portrait in an elaborate gilt and gesso frame carved with acorns used to hang in Big School. Allegedly it was burnt shortly after HGS became part of the comprehensive Dallam School.
Certainly, during the 1990s, I discovered an oil portrait of Edward Wilson, smeared with emulsion paint, under a pile of chairs in the Boarding House cellar.

Title page of the world's first Encyclopaedia, **Ephraim Chambers' " Cyclopaedia or an Universal Dictionary of Arts and Sciences"** published in 1728.
It went into many editions even before Ephraim's death in 1740. During the 1690s he was also under the tutelage of Thomas Watson at the Grammar School and hence Ephraim Chambers could be said to be HGS 's most famous scholar. He must not be confused with the Scottish publisher Robert Chambers (1802-1871) who produced another Chamber's Dictionary.

Big school between the wars.

Heversham Grammar School's **Second World War Memorial** which along with an almost identical one for the First World War, is in Big School. They show that contrary to the usual statistics HGS lost almost as many Old Boys in the Second War as in the First. The 1914 - 18 losses were 26 Old Boys and one Master. Between 1939 - 45 22 Old Boys died on active service. The fourth name on the 1939-45 list is that of my Uncle Bryan Bowker, who came from Beetham and who married my mother's sister May Rushton in 1933.

Flight Sergeant Bryan Bowker with his family Joan, Arthur and my Auntie May. Though a banker by profession, working for Barclays in the Manchester area, Bryan was a wireless enthusiast which led him to be called up before the war started to act as an RAF instructor. After four years he volunteered for active service only to be killed when his Sunderland aircraft crashed in bad weather off St. Kilda on 8th June 1944. The family was told that Bryan and the nine other crew members had been buried at sea. But 32 years later the Sunderland's wreckage was discovered along with the remains of the victims which subsequently were buried on the island, amidst much media publicity. Bryan's name is on seven War Memorials but not on that of his home village of Beetham because 'he was not living there when he was killed'.

Heversham Grammar School Advertisement 1823. When the Rev Wilson was appointed in 1822 he had recorded 'that the school I find is in a very declining state there not being more than 20 pupils all of whom are very indifferent scholars'.

Draft by the Vicar of Heversham Robert Wils[on] Evans of an **Advertisement for a 'Master'** (He[ad] Teacher) 1845. He has amended the advert for [the] previous head in 1836 by adding that the school w[as] 'one mile from the line of railway betwe[en] Lancaster and Carlisle' although the railway did [not] actually open until October 1846.

Cartoons from The School Magazine of 1957, **by Peter Brooks**, who as The Times Cartoonist and winner of many awards is currently the best known Old Hevershamian. The Mumps patient was the Head Master G.L. Willatt. He survived for nearly fifty years.

Via Dolorosa for boarders returning to HGS.
Heversham Grammar School 1920
showing the Boarding House erected 1876-78
with assembly hall block known as Big
School built c1900.

Big School in 1955 by R.K. Bingham aged 12. Heversham was
not famed for the cultivation of the fine arts. The so called cloisters
were soon obscured by an extension to the Boarders Dining Room.
Day boys eat in a separate 'canteen.'

New Library opened 1958
with, apparently, few books.

HGS c.1970. Accommodation was always poor
and these temporary wartime **prefabs** containing
the Physics and Biology Labs lasted 30 years.

Form 11F HGS Oct. 1954.

As in contemporary prisons only surnames were used, so I cannot remember the Christian names of some of my form.

Back row L to R Mashiter, Crayston, Cox, Lancaster, Lacy, Fereday, Foster, Acland, Platts.

Middle Johnson, Swindlehurst, Bingham, Form 'Master' (he was never a 'teacher') Captain A.F. Francis, Platt, Fahy, Ormerod.

Front Lemon, Thompson, Jones, Pearson, Clark.

'Captain' Francis' title derived, it was said, from a brief National Service commission as did his nickname 'Pongo'.

His incentive 'I'll beat you boy and I'll beat you hard and I'm bigger than you, Laddie' harked back further, to "Tom Brown's Schooldays".

HGS Staff 1951 Back row Messrs Hobbs, Fielding, Heap?, Meneer (son of the Rev. 'Manure' Headmaster 1909-1920), Chinn. In front Hyde, Merton?, Major, Dawson, Miss Nan Allerton-(who later married Ron Chinn), Schofield and Grimshaw.

Burt Major died in April 2007 aged nearly 104.

HGS Staff on **Founders Day 1971**. Staff with governors gather, prior to the Church service, outside the newly built Headmaster's House. They include, roughly L to R Robin Child, Alan Frostick, Rev Tom Martin, Alan Gent, Eric Rigg, Peter Benfield, Mr Davies a Governor, John Hodgson, Peter Johnson, Roger Stock, Malcolm Walker, Nan Chinn, Geoff Durham, Alan White.

Rugby team 1951. L to R Back row John Handley, Duncan Harris, Peter Stansfield, Chris Smith, David Fender, Ian Clough. Second row Peter Simpson, Malcolm McHardy, Geoff James, The Head Master, Nat Dawson, Robert Jackson, Peter Troughton, David Proctor. Seated in front John Dawson and Tony Pickthall. Nat Dawson was about to leave HGS after 12 years to take up the Headship of Epson and Ewell Grammar School, Surrey. He wears in his button hole an early hearing aid.

HGS was obsessed by sport. The current Dallam School Head was recently told by a 1950s HGS Boarder how his father received an excellent report about his son's progress until, as he was leaving, the Head casually remarked 'Oh, by the way he's not likely to pass any 'O' Levels'. Clearly prowess on the sports field took precedence over classroom competence. Similarly The Rev. E.B Kitts, Vicar of Milnthorpe recalled the look of 'utter bewilderment' on the Head's face when, after being shown acres of pitches, tennis and fives courts, an austere gymnasium, a cadet force hut and an indoor rifle range, he asked, 'Where is the music room?' There wasn't one.

12 year old HGS Rugger Players 1971. Standing L to R Ian Henderson, Stephen Maher, David Hall, Adrian Crompton, David Lord, ?, Neil McNeil, Alan Sadler, -?, Jonathan Tobias (in front Martin Chew), -Stevens. Front David Slattery, Ewan McKillop, Jonathan Fisher, ?, Andrew Colquhoun.

'1st XI'. 1957. L to R Back Row . B. Rigg, R. Jones, I. Dunbar, D. Benson, R. Markland, J. Mitchell, . Front Row A. Wilson, M. Hoggarth, E. Holloway, R. Jones. K. Wilson.

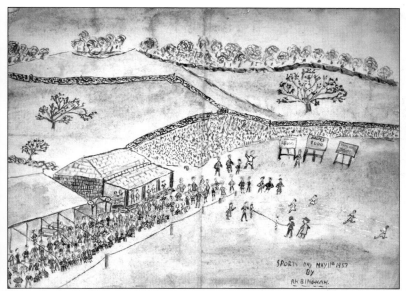

The school playing fields at **Tristrams** were situated half a mile from the school at the far end of Woodhouse Lane. Here we see, **'Sports Day 11th May 1957 by R. K. Bingham'**. I have given my house Wilson 21,000 on the easel score boards and the rival Whewell and Argles 000. About this time the PTA complained about 'Whewell always being Cock House because all the boarders were in it and so had more athletes than the other two houses put together'. In the 1930s the field up the Head, on the left, was briefly a 9 hole golf course.

HEVERSHAM HEAD GOLF CLUB.

Within 10 minutes from Heversham Church.

VISITORS' FEES:-

PER DAY	-	1/6
PER WEEK	-	5/-
PER MONTH	-	15/-

For particulars of Membership apply to:
The Hon. Secretary: J. K. JACKSON, 14, Finkle Street, Kendal; or
The Hon Treasurer: M. HIGGINBOTTOM, Whinfell, Heversham.

Advert for Heversham's transient Golf Club c.1931.

HGS Junior Fell Run winners 1961.
L to R Alan Gawith, John Bell, Martin Jackson, John Myers. The Fell Run was meant to be compulsory for all - but I skived off it six times out of seven.

HGS was very proud of its **Combined Cadet Corps** which also attracted 'sons of serving officers' to the Boarding Houses where numbers reached nearly 300 by the 1970s. Here we see a corps outing about 1980. Fourth from the left is Peter Cookson, 7th Clive Gott, 9th William Chew with teacher/officer in charge, Colin James. The CCC was disbanded when HGS became part of Dallam School whose first head John Barker reportedly said that 'a cadet force was quite inconsistent with the aims of a Comprehensive School'.

John Hancock celebrating Holy Communion outside the Old Grammar School July 1984 just before HGS merged with Milnthorpe Secondary School to become Dallam School. In the left foreground are the retiring head **John Drury** and his wife Ruth. Their humane approach to education contributed to more recent Hevershamians having happy memories of HGS.

John Drury's more civilised regime did not save him from a ducking when at the **opening of HGS's open air swimming pool** in 1970 he was thrown in by a group of his pupils. He was quickly followed by one of the masters, **John Hodgson**, caught on camera here in the split second between being slung by his hirsute tormentors and splash down - but at least his tie was on and his shirt tucked in.

Dallam School VI form was based at the Heversham Campus. The winners of **Cumbria's Young Enterprise Competition in 1989**: In front L to R Sue Greenwood, Jenny Messenger and Alison Craig. Back row Vickie Muir, Stewart Williams, Andrew Douthwaite, Kathryn Lethridge. Andrew and Alison are now married while Stewart (a boarder) married Sharon Handley of Heversham Hall. Her father began his wedding reception speech by saying 'I first became aware of Stewart when he penetrated my daughter's bedroom by means of a citizens band radio beamed from the Grammar School Boarding House...'.

Dallam School's VI Form Brochure 2007. OFSTED reported that VI Formers 'receive very good guidance and support which promotes their academic and personal development'.

Leasgill Cottage about 1980. A hundred years earlier **Miss Salkeld** ran a girls boarding school here. She was remembered for her 'firm handling of her pupils who if a drawer was left open or a blanket showed beneath the bed coverlet the drawer was emptied and the bed stripped until the lesson was learned'. That was 'education' for you!

Up to the 1980s this house straddled the Parish boundary. In the 1950s the occupants Mr and Mrs Rolf, allegedly, slept in the northern part (to the left) as the Levens side's rates were cheaper than Heversham's which they would have paid if they had used the south bedroom.

This is the only known photograph of **pupils at the Old School** which moved to Leasgill in 1891. The move followed 'typhoid breaking out amongst the infants' caused it was thought by the school's privies leaking into nearby St. Mary's Well.

Prospectus for the **Heversham Church of England School 1842** showing 'the Old School' and the Mistress' House. The school was built in the Church yard by James Gandy of Heaves in 1839 and the house was built by the Hon. Mary Howard of Levens Hall in 1841. Following a big row about whether the Mistress' Privy could be installed on consecrated ground the cottage was eventually built in an adjacent orchard.

George V and Queen Mary. Their portraits hung in the Infants classroom. Before I could read the captions I was told by another infant that they were of **God and Jesus**. The King was clearly 'Jesus' because he had a beard while the white swathed diamond encrusted figure of Majestic Mary was equally obviously 'God'.

Leasgill School c. 1899. The little girl on the extreme left in the front row is thought to be Jinnie Tarves, while Mary Proctor is next but one. "Miss Proctor" was the school's caretaker and dinner lady from 1936 - 1953.

Miss Isabella Slinger 'taken in Jan. 1905'. She was headmistress from 1901 to 1924 and was the last teacher to live in the School Cottage.

Water colour of **School Cottage c.1880** showing the mistress's washing hanging out to dry.

The school's **centenary celebrations 1991** with Jinnie Tarves now Mrs Wilson front left, behind her Peter Tyson, Mrs Linacre who as **Miss Mary Davidson** was assistant mistress from 1946-63, Betty Tyson, **Miss Nancy Wright** Headmistress 1937-77 and old boy Roger Bingham. I visited Miss Wright hours before she died in 1993 and told her 'the children send their love'; after murmuring 'thank you Roger' she lapsed into a sleep from which she never awoke.

'Miss Davidson' surprised everyone when she got married at the age of 72. She nearly achieved a Silver Wedding as she lived to be 96.

School photos provide valuable evidence for family and social historians but regrettably there is only room for a tiny selection. Here we see in about **1934** L to R Miss Dunn (later Mrs Lathom), Edna Hayton, Peter Tyson, Oliver Simpson, Edward Sisson, John Tyson, Albert Robinson, Leslie Dobson, Ruby Nelson, Mrs Mackay-head teacher. Next row. -, Jean Simpson, Edith Binnie, Gladys Hayton, Jean Park, Nancy Whitwell, Jean Strickland, Margaret Howson. Next row. J. Gregg, -, Eileen Dodson, Jean Binnie, Marjorie Bennett, Mary Bainbridge, -,Margaret Baker, Kenneth Stowe, Robert Dobson. Seated Kenneth Hemming, Alan Nelson, Eric Chamley, Billy Dawson, Frank Senogles.

The **School in 1938**. L to R back row John Pickthall, Billy Bennet, John Wild, Alan Moore, Alan Senogles, John Burch, Terry Jenkinson, Peter Handley. Second row Marie McHardy, Margaret Park, Ann Hodgson, Eileen Dobson, Margaret Howson, Jean Pattinson, Margery Dobson, Sybil Shepherd. Third row. Margaret Kitching, Brenda Guy, Elsie Bennet, Nora Bennet. In front Robin Pickthall, John Jenkinson, Billy Robinson, Tommy Bracken, ?.

The Jenkinsons were twins and so their names might be the other way round. They were Americans as their father, Wimborne Terry Jenkins, had just come to manage the newly built Libby's Milk Factory at Ackenthwaite. Blue Ridge on Woodhouse Lane was built for them and featured such trans-Atlantic luxuries as central heating and an 'ice-box' - and, I recall, they kept a beautiful white rabbit in the cellar..

A generation on: **Miss Davidson's infants class 1950**-my mother recalled my boasting that I had been promoted to 'middle top infants'.

L to R back row

Robert Cornthwaite, Hugh Miles, Ian Sisson, John East, Neville Hallmark, Michael Sisson, Roger Bingham, Anthony Harrison, Michael Barnes, Georgie (as we called him) Handley.

Middle row Dorothy Mason, Mary Lambert, Patricia Fell, Eileen Byrne, Carolyn Outhwaite, Christine Brown, Barbara Nelson.

In front Michael Wheatman, Brian Nelson, Graham Prickett, John Williams, Basil Cornthwaite, Leslie Fell, Richard Metcalf, John Mason.

Miss Wright's top class. 1951.
Back row Anne East, Bobbie Handley, Colin Townsend, Dorothy Nelson, David Chinn, Patricia Byrne, Michael Newhouse, Geoffrey Brown, Hazel Garnett.
Middle Row Anne Dawson, Raymond East, Pamela Bingham, Roger Bingham, Jane Ireland, Janet Miles, Herbert Wilson, Susan Byrne, David Brownlie, Irene Nelson, Basil Cornthwaite.
In front Valerie Jackson, Leslie Fell, Alan Richardson, Sandra Dickinson.

Leasgill School 1959. No one ever called it by its official name of Heversham C. of E. School.
L to R Back Row Keith Richardson, Susan Nicholson, Jane Byrne, Sylvia Taylor, Jonathan Hackett.
Middle Row ?, Myles Whitlock, Susan Bell, Kathleen Hodgson, Gordon Pearson, Nigel Gardner, - supply teacher?,
Front Row Geraldine Carruthers, Anthea Rushton, Barry Poselthwaite, Christopher Baines, Alma Nelson, Elizabeth Cheeseman, Antony Beck, Carol Carlson.

Hull High School-yes Hull - photographed in **July 1945** before the return home. "For the duration" of the Second World War this girls grammar school was **evacuated to Horncop** whose veranda can be seen on the right. As part of my export trade I am sending a copy of this booklet to Hull.

Back row Sheila Handy, Rosaline Cook, Joan King, Norma Scott, Gwyneth Calvert, Dorothy Palmer, Christine Chatterton, Elizabeth Dennis.

5th Row Sheila Curtiss, Sally Newgrosh, Thelma Page, Jean Alson, Pamela Lindsey, Joyce Stretford, Ann Barton, Kathleen Powell, Penny Rees, Wendy Dickinson, Audrey Kennington, Hilda Frost, Angela Shaw.

4th Row Delphine Minty, Barbara Hendy, Christine Waters, Mary Scott, Greta Proudlove, Betty Morgan, Sylvia Barber, Margaret Boys, Mary Haller, June Pool, Bridget Dawson, Joan Haulton, Angela Ely, Kay Pike. Staff Miss Ogden, Miss Hall, Mrs Price, Miss Downie, Miss Jefferson, Miss Brooks, Miss Lloyd, Mrs Hammerton, Miss Barrow, Miss Soulsby.

2nd Row Janet Murray, Margaret Killburn, Barbara Jackson, Hilary Kettlewell, Jane Jackson , Sally Good, Joan Gibson, Kathleen Stirk, Pandy LeLachuer, Mary Arrowsmith, Gwyneth Morgan, Margaret Worrall, Jean Russell, Judy Thompson, Jose LeLachuer, Judy Iveson, Jennifer Haines.

Front Row Audrey Outhwaite, Jill Spencer, June Wallace (local day girl), Angela Kilburn, Marjorie Kirkwood, Brenda Stirk, Angela Fawcett (day girl), Smith, Jill Good, Marilyn Feason, Wendy Spencer, Margaret Fearson, Barbara Jackson.

6: *Happy Times*

Cabaret at Mothers Union Party in the Athenaeum mid 1980s. L to R. Mrs Roach at the piano, Caroline Gazelle, Tom Sanderson, Joe Burgess, Molly Wallace, Audrey Rushton, Dorothy Darbyshire, Marion Douthwaite, Jenny Sisson and half behind the curtain Mac Sisson.

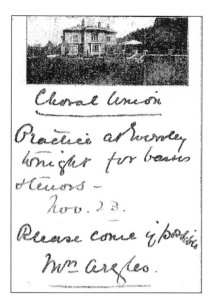

Invitation to an **Eversley Choral Union** Choir Practice issued by Agnes Argles, the Conductor, showing her Leasgill mansion from which 'the Choral' took its name. Though Mrs Argles' notice looks peremptory it was The Eversley's policy that all travelling expenses should be met by the Choral Union for members who did not have their own transport or who could not easily walk to rehearsals.

Agnes Argles

Earlier Music Making in Leasgill - **Sergeant Park's One Man Band.** A former Milnthorpe Police Sergeant he lived in retirement in his family's property on Park's Victory Row.

Cast of a **Concert** depicting Victorian Heversham photographed in the old entrance hall of the **Athenaeum 1982**.

L to R at the back Alan Frostick, ?, Valerie Chew, Dick Dyer, John Chew, George Handley, Jenny Sisson, Mac Sisson, John Hancock (playing Canon Gilbert),

Middle visiting narrator-name forgotten, Bobby Shackleford, ?) Lois Dias, Ruth Drury, John Drury, Ray Sisson.

Towards the front. John Bates, Martha Bates (writer and producer), Roger Bingham as Mr. Argles, Tom Sanderson.

In front Sharon Handley, Mary Holmes, Margaret Hancock.

Wartime Dick Whittington, Athenaeum c.1944. The cast was drawn from the Heversham Village Players with assisted talent from Milnthorpe and other villages. L to R back row, Bill Dawson, Mrs Henley, George Brownson, Tommy Cross, Arthur Camm, Mary Hodgson, Dorothy Stainton, Ferdie Casson, Mary Proctor, Edith Crossley, Hilda Cummings, Mary Thompson, Josie Wood, Middle row Marjorie Thompson, Eileen Fothergill, Margaret Cross, Margaret Gould, Jean Palmer, Gladys James, Vera Webster, Audrey Taylor, ?, Betty Douthwaite. In front Marion Sadler, Sheila Wheatman, Gillian Taylor, Wilma Taylor, Betty Tait, Edith Ryles, Anne Lister, Pauline Thompson, Frances Moore (just behind), Pauline Barber, Harold Hird - as the cat.

George Leigh Brownson as the Emperor and Hilda Cummings as his Princess in the Athenaeum's 'Dick Whittington' 1944. Mr Brownson was reputed to be a millionaire which may account for a total lack of wartime austerity in his costume - except for his bedroom slippers. He had a sprung dance floor in his house 'Collina' on The Princes Way. His sceptre doubtless came from his collection of oriental artefacts. At the house sale of his furnishings in 1965 my mother bought a chinese vase for 10s. We were all greatly excited when we found a note inside reading, '1921 Hswan Dah's Reign, this vase is 240 years old and very valuable'. But alas, the 'Antiques Roadshow' decreed that it was a reproduction 'worth very little'. At Heversham Church a small chalice of 'Icelandic design' used at 8am Holy Communions commemorates Mr Brownson's services as Churchwarden.

Mr Brownson's Chalice.

Mr Brownson's vase.

The cast of 'Poor Jenny She is weeping' photographed by Mac Sisson in the Athenaeum 10th October 1986.
Produced by Doreen Morgan the repertoire included Victorian games, songs and music along with selections from 'Oliver'.
L to R Back row Brian Barden, Chris Bethell, Andrew Gardiner, Steve Beatty, John Drury, Gordon Capstick, Geoff Bethell (head of Leasgill School), Trevor Slade. Third row Enid Ayling, Neil Shaw, Chris Bethell, Ruth Whittaker, Kate Warren, Margaret Hesmondhalgh, Vanessa Warren, Karen Barden, Isobel Butler-Cole.
Second row Melanie Waskiel, Hannah Mowat, Rachel Capstick, Ben Barden (who stole the show with his plaintive rendition of "Where is Love?"), Freya Mowat, Nina Capstick, Duncan Thompson, Abigail Watson, Graham Baines.
Front row Sarah Hesmondhalgh, Kerry Townshend, Sarah Greaves, Jenny Sisson, Helen Greaves, William Baverstock, Paul Capstick, Philip Sisson, Jennifer Coatesworth.

George Handley and Kathleen Byrne cheerfully survey the **Athenaeum's squalid kitchen** shortly before it was replaced with a more up to date and hygienic 'servery' c.1979.

South Westmorland Stage and Screen Society's presentation of **Cast** 1949. Phyllis Bingham brings in the flowers wearing the uniform of her own maid, Annie Cheeseman, who came from Hincaster. SWSS, formed by a break away group from Milnthorpe Dramatics, which included my mother, was founded in 1948. It performed at Heversham for 30 years until the Society obtained its own Heron Theatre at Beetham.

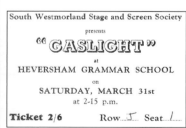

South Westmorland Stage and Screen Society
presents
"GASLIGHT"
at
HEVERSHAM GRAMMAR SCHOOL
on
SATURDAY, MARCH 31st
at 2-15 p.m.
Ticket 2/6   Row J Seat 1

Cora Dawson, Charles Nickel and Phyllis Bingham in **Gas Light 1951**. SWSS took pride in authentic sets and costumes.

HEVERSHAM BOY PLAYERS
SOUTH WESTMORLAND STAGE & SCREEN SOCIETY

ALICE IN WONDERLAND

By LEWIS CARROLL

(stage version by Norman Dawson)

December 9th to 16th, 1950.

Programme 3d.

Alice, Barry Armstrong being courted by Peter Bruggen as the **White Knight**.

1950 Programme. 'Alice in Wonderland' was performed jointly by Heversham Grammar School's 'Boy Players' and SWSS. Produced by HGS's Headmaster Nat Dawson, there were 45 in the cast and spectacular sets and costumes. Alice was played on alternative nights in the two week run by Robin Acland and Barry Armstrong. The 'Club' boy (on the programme) was played by Peter Lightburn, whose father was editor of the Westmorland Gazette which printed full and, justifiably, laudatory reviews of the production.

Kitchen Scene. L to R Jimmy Giles as the Cheshire Cat, Mary Harvey as the Cook, Robin Acland as Alice, Zuleika Ireland as the Duchess beating the Pig Baby who I think is a doll though the programme states that 'it' was played by Janet Dawson. Regrettably this is the only photo I've found of **Miss Harvey** one of Heversham's most unforgettable characters famed for her intellectual conversation, way out costumes and her housekeeping which was so chaotic that everybody said she was typecast for the cook in 'Alice'.

```
              SOUTH  WESTMORLAND
          STAGE  AND  SCREEN  SOCIETY

                    presents

FLASHES FROM "ALICE IN WONDERLAND"
       A short film record of scenes from the
stage production of "Alice in Wonderland"
given in 1950 jointly by the Heversham Boy
Players and the S.W.S.S.S.    Scenes shot in
colour are intermingled with black-and-white.

COAL TO GAS
       A documentary film made by the Skegness
Photographic and Cine Society.

TIME TO CONSIDER
       Humorous treatment of a road-safety
theme by the Fourfold Film Society.

    * * *  Interval of ten minutes  * * *

MORE THAN A MATCH
       First public presentation of the Soci-
ety's initial venture in film production:
a comedy-documentary of village life in a
South Westmorland setting.

HOLIDAYS IN SUN AND SNOW
       A travel documentary filmed in Switzer-
land.

          _____

       To cater for 'bus travellers this pro-
gramme is timed to end at about 8.50 p.m.
```

Film night programme 1952. Though petrol was by now off the ration performances and all other public events were geared to fit in with bus timetables.

Tristams 1951. Scene from **'More than a Match'** a silent film directed for SWSS by Nat Dawson and Alex Lyon. Other scenes were filmed in Beetham, Heversham, Holme and Milnthorpe.

Crowd scene from 'More than a Match' 1951. The little girl in front is Jane Ireland. The striped lady behind is her mother who was addressed by three separate names: her real name of Zuleika (yes really), Freda - the feminine form of her husband's name Freddie and 'Pinkie' after a part she played in an SWSS production. But at the back extreme left is me standing up, already bored stiff with Cricket. Note the period touches - all the ladies are in dresses, the kiddies bike has mudguards and I'm wearing a tie.

SWSS Garden Party at Plumtree Hall 1954.
Back row Freddie Ireland, Betty Harrower, Noreen Mellor, Harold
Mellor. Second row Aileen Clark, Phyllis Bingham, Henry Dobson,
Norton Wayne 'the famous stage and screen star', Mrs Wayne, Mrs
Knibbs, Annie Hutchinson.
In front, Clare, Neville and Stephen Hallmark.

South Westmorland Stage & Screen Society

A GARDEN FETE

to be held at

Plumtree Hall, Heversham

(by kind permission of Miss Watson)

commencing at

2-30 p.m. on Saturday, July 24th

will be opened by

Mr. Naunton Wayne

of Stage and Screen fame, by kind permission
of The Royalty Theatre, Morecambe, where he
is appearing from July 19th to 24th in—
" Count your Blessings" by Ronald Jeans

Baby Show at 3-30 p.m.
for " Women's Pictorial " Guinea photograph prizes
Ladies Ankle Competition.
Children's Sketch   Punch & Judy Show
Children's Dancing Display, Films, Stalls, Side-shows, etc.
Teas and Ices.

Admission 6d.   Car Park Free

(If wet, the Fete will be held in
The Athenaeum, Leasgill)

Holdsworths. Sandside. Milnthorpe.

The Garden Party poster.

Scene from the Grammar School's Production of **St. Joan, 1961**. Edward Acland as
Robert de Baudricourt bullies his steward Roger Bingham. Bernard Shaw described the
steward as being 'a down trodden worm scanty of hair and scanty of flesh being the sort
of man whom age cannot wither because he has never bloomed' –so I was obviously type
cast. Subsequently, as members of different parties, Edward and I continued our combat
on the District and County Councils.

Plumtree Hall Barnado's Junior Helpers League Garden Party boosted by evacuees, 1940. L to R Margaret Hodgson, evacuee, evacuee, Daisy Jenkins, Margaret Park, Jean Pennington, Betty Proctor, evacuee, evacuee. Front row evacuee, evacuee, evacuee, Anne Hodgson, Audrey Proctor, evacuee, Sitting evacuee, Judy Thompson, Anne Lister, Peter Thompson, evacuee. Nearly 70 years later Peter recalled that his role was 'Simple Simon'. Heversham's 'Dr Banana's' raised money for the children of Barrows Green Orphanage including funds 'to kit out' young Barnado's emigrants bound for Australia, a cause now widely held to have been contrary to 'human rights'.

May Pole Dancers at Plumtree Hall 1959. L to R Lynda Bennett, ?, Christine Wilson, Gilliam Parkin, Christine Wilson, Miles Whitlock, Kathleen Hodgson, Susan Bell, Christine Proctor, Anthea Rushton, Terry Bennett. In front Hilary Sisson, ? Derek Bennett, John Hodgson, ?, ?, Angela Dobson, Kathleen Bowness, Ailsa Jackson, kneeling down Jane Byrne.

A happy picture of **Miss Daphne Cunningham** at Threave on The Prince's Way in 1983, with some of the dolls collected by herself and her sister Kay which they exhibited to raise thousands of pounds for charity. Daphne was a long serving Matron of Kendal Hospital while Kay, aka Major Cunningham was one of the highest ranking women's officers in the Second World War.

Major Kay Cunningham

Brownies, Guides and Scouts involved most local youth in the mid 20th Century. **Heversham Brownies in 1955.** L to R. Back row Caroline Outhwaite, Eileen Byrne, Jennifer Jackson, Linda Jackson, Mary Lambert. Front Row Barbara Nelson, Christine Wilson, Dot Mason, Christine Brown

When they really did look the part. The **Heversham Scout troop c.1940** on the Head L to R back row Toby Proctor, Bill Dawson, Leslie Dobson, Middle row Frank Senogles, Kenneth Flemming, Front row Eric Proctor, Billy Dawson, Norris Chamley, in front John Dawson.

Heversham Guides camping at Windermere c.1934.

Heversham Scouts camping at Rusland, 1955. John Tyson, Norris Chamley, Ian Sisson, Michael Wheatman, John East, Mike Hodgson, in the smoke John Baines.

Pamela wore white stilettos when I gave her away to Andrew Thurnhill in April 1964. Mother made the wedding dress which cost £4 while the Heaves Hotel's reception bill for 100 guests was £83. The average wedding bill in 2007 is said to be £17,000.

The Wedding of Scout Master John Tyson to Brown Owl Nancy Whitwell 1951. Peter Tyson is behind the happy couple with on the left Dorothy Nelson, Herbert Wilson, Diana Lambert, Janet Miles. -, Irene Nelson. On the right Jane Ireland, Pamela Bingham, Mary Lambert, Valerie Jackson and, we think, Eileen Byrne. Pamela is staring at Nancy's brown laced shoes. She thought that Nancy had been rather 'over sensible' and she never forgot that 'she didn't even wear nylons'. John and Nancy both served the village and the Church all their days. Living on the door step they were responsible, among a myriad of good works, for locking the church which, happily, is always open in the daytime. As a Lay Reader I was privileged to preach at both their funerals choosing 'Be Prepared' as my text for John, and for Nancy 'I would rather be a gate keeper at the door of my father's house than dwell in the temples of the ungodly'.

Captain Josceline Bagot M.P. of Levens Hall escorts his daughter Marjorie to her wedding to James Winstanley Cropper (of Burneside Paper Mills) 12th September 1912. The little girls are strewing roses along the churchyard path while their Mammas appear to be wearing gardens on their heads.

Two more photos of Heversham's most sumptuous wedding. The list of their wedding presents nearly filled a page in The Westmorland Gazette.

MR. AND MRS. J. W. CROPPER LEAVING THE CHURCH.

MRS. BAGOT ENTERING THE CHURCH.

Hogg. Kendal

Wedding Party at Milton Moor c.1907, home of Thomas Inman, Churchwarden of Heversham. Back row Thomas Thwaites, Lizzie, Mary, Mr Airey,
In front, Groom Christopher Robert Inman and his Bride Alice Airey.

Heversham Girls Friendly Society 1927 photographed outside Springfield , village street, the home of Miss Bannerman who is the smiling lady with the tight necklace in the centre. The lady in Edwardian garb is thought to be Mrs Lloyd of Woodhouse. Only a few 'girls' can now be named-hence all the blanks.
Back row L to R -,Sarah Strickland, Sylvia Allan, Miss Bannerman, -, Mrs Lloyd?, Miss Wild, Isobel Strickland, Mary Proctor.
Front Row-, -, Lillian, Molly Sisson, Nellie, Eleanor, Lilly Proctor –later Mrs Lister whom at the time was Miss Bannerman's maid. She later helped her sister Mary as Leasgill School caretaker

and as a dinner lady. The photograph illustrates the rapid change in **dress fashion** from the Milton Moor wedding of only 20 year's earlier and may also be compared with the dress of the girl bell ringers of 30 years later.

Here we see a later generation of church youngsters in the **Nativity Play c.1984.** Although it is relatively new this photo has been by far the hardest one to name, owing partly to the dish cloth disguises, but also because several actors came from out of the Parish while others, having grown up, have moved away. Regrettably our young people are Cumbria's biggest export. But this is the best that a combined effort can do: Top Marina Barratt, then L to R David Brooks, Beverly Elliot, Rachel Capstick, Sarah Hesmondhalgh, then Clive Slade, Johnny Holmes, Derek Van Broek, ?, James Grey. Then ?, ?, Susie Wilson, James Holland, Andrew Hancock? In front David Sowerby, Simon Johnson, Richard Warren, Jonathan Roach, ?.

Founder Members at **Heversham Women's Institute's 25th Birthday** celebrations at The Athenaeum 1954. Until a separate Milnthorpe WI was formed in 1946 there was a joint Institute for both villages-hence several Milnthorpe Ladies are in the picture. L to R. Mrs Hales, ?, Mrs Pickthall, Miss Scott, Mrs Jessie Thompson, Miss Lloyd cutting the cake, Mrs P.G. Thompson, Mrs Sheldon, Miss Hilda Austin, Mrs Ladell, ?, Mrs Hyde, Mrs Sisson, Miss Proctor.

Heversham has always celebrated national events in fine style. Here we see village lads **building the 1911 Coronation Bonfire** on top of the Head.

The finished fire 1911.
This photo was illustrated in the official book of 'Coronation Bonfires 22 June 1911' presented to King George V. No one measured its height but Heversham has always contended that our fire was higher than Milnthorpe's 35ft pyre on Haverbrack.

An iconic Heversham Photograph: **The Silver Jubilee Bonfire May 1935.** L to R Jim Sisson, Jean Simpson, Edith Binnie, Leslie Dobson, Oliver Simpson, Jean Binnie, Margaret Howson, Bill Dobson, Ena Bousfield, Billy Dawson, Frank Senogles, John Burch, and John Dawson.

VE Day Bonfire 1945. R to L R. Mashiter, J. Tarves, John Handley jnr., John Handley, F. Birkett, W. Dawson, J. Chamley, Mr Howson, J. Stowe, lying down J. Stowe jnr. Regrettably there are no photographs of the 1953 Coronation Bonfire which I, as the youngest Boy Scout lit along with Leslie Fell and Girl Guide Valerie Jackson.

The 1977 Bonfire. It was built lower down the Head rather than in the traditional place on the summit - but it was still a good blaze. In 1953 over twenty other **Coronation Beacons** could be seen in a necklace of twinkling lights stretching from the Howgills in the east via the Lancashire heights, through the Furness Fells round to the Lakeland mountains far off on the northern skyline.

Darren, Derek and Stuart Richardson in front of the **Queen's Silver Jubilee Bonfire, June 1977**. Darren followed in my footsteps because as the youngest helper he lit the fire.

Although no-one took a photo in 1953 when I lit the Coronation Bonfire, I was caught on camera at the **Golden Jubilee Bonfire in June 2002.** Because I was Chairman of South Lakeland District Council I was asked to light the fire. Here we see me in the SLDC chain (which rumour said I even wore with my pyjamas) on top of the Head just before the match was struck, along with John Cushnie, Bill Gott and John Coom.

'Mr. Handley's Field', between the village street at Leasgill and The Princes Way, with Dallam Bus in the background. This is either the Official **Victory Celebrations** of 1946 **or** the first **Children's Day 1947**. In any event the 'wot no coupons' display dates the scene to the era of austerity.

Favoured by the weather
Children's Day at Heversham 1951

Children's Day and sports held in a field adjoining Prince's Way by kind permission of Mr. J. Handley commenced with a short open-air service led by the vicar (Rev. W. A. Cleghorn).

A fancy dress parade attracted many entrants. Brigadier General Audland and Mrs. Audland of Ackenthwaite, Milnthorpe, being the judges. Results: G i r l s, Prettiest: (in order of merit) Pamela Bingham. "Eastern Lady." Patricia Fell "Bo-Peep," Janet Miles "Gipsy." Boys: Most Handsome Roger Bingham "Rizzio," John East "Red Indian." Peter Corless "W. G. Grace." Girls', Comic: Margaret Atkinson Anne Lister, "Darby and Joan," Jane Ireland "Spring Cleaning." Irene N e l s o n "Punchinello." Boys Comic: Derek Richardson "Father on Night Duty," J. Markland. Raymond East, "Baby in Pram." Most Original: (not prize winners), Geoffrey B r o w n. "Feather Bed Farmer". Ann Foster "Festival of Britain." Keith Richardson "Grow more Food."

Money left over from the Victory Celebrations was used to start an **Annual Children's Day**. Here we see the **Fancy Dress winners in 1951**. L to R. Back row three HGS boarder, then May Atkinson as Darby to Anne Lister's Joan. In front John East, Pamela Bingham, Jane Ireland, Irene Nelson, Janet Miles, Barbara Fell, Roger Bingham – as Rizzio (Who? He was Mary Queen of Scots lover. I've no idea why I depicted him), Colin Townsend wheeling Big Baby Raymond East. In front Derek Richardson, Peter Corless.

Have I no shame? My mother kept this cutting; she is responsible for the underlined part, which contrary to all appearances, she regarded as important.

A politically incorrect **Michael Barnes c.1954.**

c.1955. The field with Frank Varley's new bungalow in the background. Frank's was the first home to be built on **'millionaires row,'** so called because they were the first private houses to be built after the relaxation of post-war building licenses. Here we see L to R Anne Foster, Lillian James and Margaret James while Valerie Jackson sprints to the right.

Children's Day prize presentation c. 1959.
On stage L to R. Lillian James, Jennifer Jackson, P.G. Thompson, Granddad John Handley, Nancy Tyson, Ray Sisson. Linda Bennet stands up below stage right.

Mid 1950's **Tug o' War** between Heversham and Hincaster.

On the **1947 Children's Day** Anne Foster won first prize as 'Mary had a Little Lamb' which her husband Eddie Galbraith thinks must have 'been a suffolky sort of thing and not a mule'. In 2007 Anne was also at the Sports but 'hadn't realised she should be on the veterans photograph'.

During the 1970's the village sports transferred to the Bottom Pitch at HGS. Here we see **Silver Jubilee Fancy Dress** entries Malcolm McHardy and Billy Douthwaite.

George and the Dragon Georgie Handley St. George, Dragon Derek Warwick with a very young Tony Barnes and dad, Michael Barnes.

Line up at Heversham Children's Sports 16th June 2007 of some of the "children" who had been at the first Children's Day 60 years previously. L to R George Handley, Roger Bingham, Terry Proctor, Jean Makin, nee Pattinson, Brenda Saddler, nee Guy, Dorothy Slater, nee Atkinson, Michael Sisson, Margaret Walden, nee Webster, Doris Henderson, nee Webster, Anne Hamer, nee Lister. **Where _did_ the time go?**

The Bleasdale Beadles seen outside the Heversham Hotel c.1953. Behind the huntsman on the left are Dud Allen, Harriet Proctor and Mrs Farey. In the centre is Mrs Nancy Metcalfe-Gibson with to the right John Cross, ?, Jack Nanson, Dallam Tower Agent, George Black, Tom Farrington, Dallam Tower Huntsman. **Mrs Metcalfe-Gibson** came from Killington but forty years later she retired to a Heversham care home. She then became a very familiar villager as, bent nearly double, chain smoking and supported on two sticks she hobbled round all the lanes. Heedless of innumerable warnings - even from the police - she always used the middle of the road. But, to every drivers surprise she died in her own bed and at an enormous age. Even so, ten years later, I still instinctively sound my car horn by the Woodhouse Lane Bridge where I frequently met and narrowly missed Heversham's notorious - if gallant - veteran pedestrian.

Bobby Handley holds **one of Sam's victims**. Kneeling to the right are Peter Handl[ey?] and Derek Ward. The four men behind are Sam, Jim Barnes, Robin Wallace and Sam[s] son Gordon. In front to the right of Bobby are Robert Wilson, Terry Proctor, Der[ek] Hartley, just behind from the right are Kenneth Barnes, Alan Richardson, J Giles ([a] HGS Boarder). The three men at the back from the right are Bill Dawson, HGS Board[er] called Crayston?, Mr Hartley. Robin Wallace was not the same person as the 'Engli[sh] Cezanne' who painted the frontispiece of this book. 'Our' Robin was the manager [of] Sandside Quarry and also an expert wild fowler - hence his cocked 12 bore.

Sam Birkett with part of a famous (or infamous) cull. In the winter of 1953 Sam shot in one afternoon five foxes on Heversham Head. I can remember him parading them past Leasgill School bus queue as he went to celebrate at The Heversham Hotel. I thought he was a gamekeeper but the reverse of that occupation was more likely to be the case. Although the Magistrate Court records describe him as a stonemason, Sam was a Tailor. Fifty years later Terry Proctor recalls 'He sat crossed legged in the tailors shop, making moleskin trousers and we used to help him feed the strange looking brightly coloured cockerels in the Quarry. He never told us why they sometimes looked so strange'.

Sam's Tailors Shop in the grounds of Highfield, Leasgill, with Sandra Elder on 'Izzy' and Helen Wore on 'Lennox'. There is still a large skylight in the roof to light the upper floor workroom which was approached by a ladder from the shop.

128

A traditionally trimmed **fighting cock**. Sam's cocks were more like bantams and were plucked so that they had 'strange' bare shoulders with a thick ruff left round the neck. Their mash feed had an enticingly sweet aroma as even during the austere 1940s it was laced with port so that the game birds could 'feed like fighting cocks'. Unfortunately for Sam the Police knew about his strange birds.

The Cock Pit, one of the largest in the land was the setting for Shrove Tuesday 'Mains' held by Grammar Boys who had to pay cockpence to the Master. This practice provided the name for the otherwise ambiguous title of the School's subsequent **Cock House competitions**. The bench on the right was installed with others on Heversham Head by Mr and Mrs Alston of Milnthorpe Hill in memory of their only son, a naval officer who lost his life in the **'Affray' submarine disaster** in the English Channel in 1951.

£34 IN FINES FOLLOW WHITBARROW SCAR COCK-FIGHT

Kendal Police Court Story: Defence Solicitor on Modern "Effeminacy"

Westmorland Gazette headline for April 15th 1933 reporting the sequel to a police raid on a cockfight 'main' in Whitbarrow Woods. The twelve accused (who had to be seated in the Police Court jury box) included Frank and Sam Birkett from Leasgill and James Duncan, a gardener whose wife kept Heversham's village shop. He claimed that he had gone to the woods to collect pea sticks. They were sentenced to a month's imprisonment or a £3 fine. They all took the 'option'. Also convicted were Edward Batten ('Ben') Edwards, gamekeeper to the Drews of Eversley House, Leasgill, and Linton Inman of Lyth. Allegedly 'Lint's' brother Frank evaded arrest by hiding in a badger set. Ben's grandson Eric Proctor, who is now Heversham's oldest native born resident, then aged eight, was also present and recalls how Ben kept the police talking on the back door step while other cockers escaped through the front door. None of them learned their lesson and Sam Birkett and his cronies were convicted again in the 1950s when post war inflation had pushed the fines up to £10. There are now fewer rumours that 'the old sport' still goes on. But I still remember a local rhyme **"heaven - born boys that in cocking delight, are ever true-hearted and constant in fight"**.

Cock spurs. In the 1933 case the defence council 'alleged that it was more cruel for cocks to fight without steel spurs, because those spurs inflicted a clean wound which, if not fatal, healed quickly'.

Weather Cock at Grievegate, Leasgill. It is set on a turret above the former boiler room for the Eversley greenhouses. The figure is that of **Ben Edwards** and purports to show him shooting left handedly.

R.D. Humber. Bobby Humber's family was the last to live at Elm Lawn before it became The Heversham Hotel. The decor of its cocktail bar, called 'The Cockpit', featured a pair of birds spurred for action. These had, of course, been reared for exhibition purposes only. Bobby was a founder member of the Westmorland Wild Fowler's Association, whose members shoot native and migrant birds around the Kent Estuary. According to his publisher's blurb, Bobby combined "a love of wildlife and birds, with a true countryman's lack of sentimentality and he enjoys bird watching, fell foxhunting, shooting and fishing".

William Strickland at Leasgill c. 1950 with a kestrel which was killed by a mother hen, "a cross between a game cock and a Rhode Island Red hen", after the predator had attacked her chicks. The story is related by R.D. Humber in his "Game Cock and Countryman" (Cassell & Company 1966) which is filled with partly apocryphal tales of cockfighting around Heversham in the mid twentieth century when the 'sport' had already been illegal for a hundred years.

Cartoon c. 1941, by Phyllis Bingham depicting some of her husband **Dr. Ken Bingham's extra-medical activities.** What was said of Bobby Humber applied equally to my father who in his brief period as a local GP spent almost as much time killing things out on the mosses as he spent being compassionate in his surgery or on his rounds.

In the **Barnes' Farmyard, Moss Side c.1955.** Surrounding a dead badger which was then a rare and unprotected creature are L to R James Wilson, Tom Farrington, Dallam Tower Gamekeeper called in to deal with the situation, Jim Barnes, Keith Clement, Brian Shaw, -?, Roy Semple, Malcolm Robinson, -?, John Cross. Kneeling-?, Mike Barnes. Despite appearances this is not a Badger baiting scene but an-almost- legitimate cull. The story goes that the badger had dug a deep set under a hedge which the lambs got through only to be worried by 'Mr Brock'.

THE POLECAT OR "FOUMART"

Polecat or pine marten or foulmart or 'foumart'. They were once common around Heversham and are said to exist still on Whitbarrow Scar. 'Smelling like a bag of foumarts' remains a local expression for a big stink. Historically, hunting them and other vermin was a lucrative pastime. In 1809 Heversham Church Wardens paid 2s 6d for a bag of 14 foumarts' heads. 200 years earlier they paid 'Anthony Chambers 2s 10d for a fox head, 4 catts and 2 brocks'.

Keen gardeners Bill Strickland and Jimmy Frear from Leasgill admire (or criticise) entries in the Milnthorpe and District Flower Show c.1967.

Plumtree Hall with Plumtree Bank behind showing extensive kitchen gardens and also a ploughed field which forty years later is less common in our by now predominantly grazing landscape c.1960.

'Spice', John and Mavis Robinson in their **garden at Lower Rowell.** Their garden is the first in Heversham to be included in the **NGS 'Yellow Book'.** Though the garden is 'Olde Worlde' and the house is Tudor the farm is bang up to date as the Robinson's have just (2007) installed the district's first 'Robot Milking Machine'.

Horncop c.1955 in Mrs Ellwood's day showing the half acre of kitchen garden cared for by her gardener Birkett Mattinson, who like 'Starkie' the chauffeur was always addressed by his surname. It was from the roof of the loggia seen at the front of the house that burglars twice broke in while the household was asleep, causing a huge sensation in the district.

In 1930 Heversham's old tennis court became a **bowling green**. Miss Watson of Plumtree Hall rolled the first bowl. Frank Dickinson owner of The Heversham Hotel to the left with raised arm, James Duncan stands with folded arms while a svelte, all in white, Hermione Drew looks on.

Heversham has rarely, if ever, had a village football team but there have been **ad hoc cricket** sides Here see Heversham's Team at Sedgwick 1970s. L to R back row Mrs Bingly-umpire, Keith Richardson, Stan Aikrigg, Andrew Matthews, Andrew Hamer, Martin Jackson, Michael Hodgson, ?, In front L to R. Len Earl, Mark Lein-Webber, John Chew, Derek Richardson.

Heversham Badminton Club reached the Final of the Albert Pearson Knockout Competition in the mid 1970's. L to R, back row Peter Barker, Everley Buckley, John Bell. In front Barbara Casey, Margaret Hesmondhalgh, Judith Edmondson.

After the Grammar School Courts were opened in 1959 Tennis figured prominently in the village with the Heversham team winning the **Westmorland Men's trophy in 1975**. L to R David Zair, Jack Thomas, John Bell, Peter Townshend, Alan Thomas, Terry Camm, Antony Hesmondhalgh.

Heversham Church bell ringers early 1950s. L to R Back Row Tony Wood, Robin Birley, Ian Sisson, Michael Sisson, Peter Wood, Bill Dawson, Peter Handley; in front Margaret Nelson, Jean Richardson, Dorothy Nelson. Robin, a lawyer, who lived in Heversham was a member of the famous family of archaeologists who excavated Vindolanda on Hadrian's Wall. Robin made the ringers mats (seen in the photo) which are still going strong after 50 years of ringing the changes.

Happy Times in the Belfry. The team has just completed the **Millennium Peal** on **New Year's Day 2000**. L to R. Back Row George Handley, Ian Sisson. In front Doreen and Chris Baines, Angela Andrews, Robin Sisson.

Heversham Hand Bell Ringers perform at a Rogation Day Service at John and Jean Sowerby's Deepthwaite Farm c.2001.

Time Marches On-or-Change and Decay is all around I see-**repainting the Church Clock 1995**. Hence, in, say, 2057 someone will have to compile an updated 'Memories of Heversham'. In 1930 J.F. Curwen stated in the dedication to his 'Heversham with Milnthorpe' at **'every house where enquiries have been made, a warm welcome and friendly chat have made, not only this history possible, but the time spent delightful'. This has been my own happy experience and I trust that Heversham's hospitable tradition will persist for future chroniclers.**

And finally my favourite Heversham photograph which Mac Sisson saved from the Athenaeum's collection of glass slides. **Going to Milnthorpe Circus** probably about 1890, but no one can now remember exactly and the elephant, though he or she would not forget, is no more.

ACKNOWLEDGEMENTS

May I offer a big thank you to the very many people who provided information, illustrations and practical help with photography and computers? I am sorry that I cannot remember everybody but the following readily spring to mind: Tommy Allen, Sir Christopher Audland, Hal Bagot, Brian and Diane Barnes, Michael and Maureen Barnes, Alan and Linda Baverstock, John Bell, Agnes Bennett, Grant Branwell, Dr Brian Brooks, Peter Brooks, Carnmor Print (Michael Evans, Winston and Michelle Munro, Clare Wilkinson), Gordon and Mary Capstick, Norris Chamley, Hilda Cochrane, Cumbria Archives and Library Services, Denise Cummings, Daphne Cunningham, John and Valerie Chew, Dr Bill and Marion Douthwaite, Neil Dowker, Jaqui and Mark Edmondson, Dick Etheridge, Farnell Photography, Jaqui Fay, Anne Galbraith, Ron Gerard, Bill and Anita Gott, Nick and Tim Griffiths, Paul Grout, Anne Hamer, Canon John and Margaret Hancock, George and Jean Handley, John Handley, Sheila Healey, Geoff and Gina Harrison, Antony and Margaret Hesmondhalgh, Heversham PCC, Alan and Eileen Hodgson , John Hodgson, RFG Hollett and Son, Ailsa Hulme, Steve Holdup, Jennifer Horton, David Inman, Colin and Hilary James, Peter and Otalia Johnson, Dr Anne Lendrum, Olive Mason, Barry Morgan, Andrew Moses, Brian and Margaret Nelson, Tony Parker, Bob Parratt, Audrey Phillips, Hazel Phillips, Bernard and Karen Pickthall, Steven and Drusilla Pickthall, Eric and Harriet Proctor, Terry Proctor, Dr Ian Richards, Margaret Rendell, Derek Richardson, John and Mavis Robinson, Frank and Margery Rockcliffe, Jean Shuttleworth, Ray Sisson, Robin Sisson, Jean and John Sowerby, Billy and Christine Strickland, Sheila Tauber, Joyce Thompson, Juliette Townsend, Martin Tyson, Larry Walling, Roger Whittaker, Herbert Wilson, and the Rev. Sue Wilson.

N.B. In accordance with current practice all groups of children illustrated in this book date from before c.1986.